"It is no use saying, 'we are doing our best.' You have got to succeed in doing what is necessary." —Winston Churchill

INTRO TO FAILURE

How the American Higher Education System is collapsing

William W. Pacwa

Augustus
Plebeian
Press

Intro to Failure: How the American Higher Education System is Collapsing
By William W. Pacwa

ISBN: 978-0-578-74475-9
First Edition, August 2020

Cover art by Rocko Spigolon
Edited by Dale P. and Avner L.

To request permissions, submit inquiries, or request more information, contact the Author with all correspondence sent to the relevant addresses below.

PO BOX 1323
Gallatin, TN 37066
United States of America
www.augustusplebeianpress.com
W.pacwa@gmail.com

To my benevolent Creator, who enlightens me in times of darkness.

Table of Contents

Issues with Institutions of Higher Education

"To tell you the truth, though, I still haven't made up my mind whether I shall publish at all. Tastes differ so widely, and some people are so humorless, so uncharitable, and so absurdly wrong-headed, that one would probably do far better to relax and enjoy life than worry oneself to death trying to instruct or entertain a public which will only despite one's efforts, or at least feel no gratitude for them." —Sir Thomas More, Utopia

With the advancement of groundbreaking technology that makes it easier to communicate and obtain information, why has the basic model of teaching within the American higher education system not fundamentally changed? During my time in university, the old school format of lecture, notes, and reading assignments in a classroom was the dominant form of teaching. Throughout college, I found myself learning more from documentaries on YouTube and other informative sites on the internet rather than the lectures from professors. The internet and online formats were only used sparsely in class, usually being the backup to the information that was taught in the classroom.

Seemingly, the only technological advancements in higher education are students taking notes on laptops and the professor sometimes using the projector to display talking points. This is only going to get worse as technology advances and universities choose to change little. Almost everything in society has been revolutionized by advanced technology from camera equipped doorbells to self-driving cars, but the model of teaching that was designed to produce factory workers in the early industrial era has not changed.

Why has the country's university apparatus, once thought of as the golden ticket to a better life, not provided graduates with the same opportunities as those who have come before them? Many college students graduate into an unsympathetic economy that does not value their degree as much as the graduates themselves value it. They believe that because they graduate from a university that they will be instantly blessed with a six-figure salary. Many of my cohorts were under this delusional impression, and as a result, they think their massive student loan debt is not a big problem. However, it is a problem. Graduates get kicked in the teeth when they try to find employment, and they are unsurprisingly shocked when their expectations are not manifested. Why do thousands of jobs that historically never required a four-year education now demand a college degree? Nearing the end of my time in college, I began looking for jobs and was surprised to find that simple jobs like working for a political campaign or other business offices required a degree even though it was not inherently needed to perform the job. Someone who is highly intelligent could perform the job just as well as someone with a college diploma. There was nothing that a college education inherently provided like requisite skills that were needed for these jobs. Moreover, there are jobs in the economy that do not even require a college degree that pay significantly more, especially jobs in vocational studies. What is the remedy for this type of skills gap in the labor market? I knew many students who were naturally industrious but decided to attend university because they thought it was a financially better choice. This is not the case for everyone, and some people would be better served following a path outside university in a vocational skills career.

Why has the price of a college education dramatically increased at a faster rate than health care or energy? Compared to past generations, I paid significantly more for my college education even though I did not gain much in the process. What's more is that my tuition was low compared to students I knew from other private universities who were paying double my tuition costs.

Why do students spend valuable time on general education requirements that have nothing to do with their specific field of study? Thankfully, I fulfilled the university's science requirement, but if I had not gotten out of that requirement, I would have had to take two science courses as a declared political science major. The university, however, forced me to take a math class which was calculus; I thought this was the best option as I just finished pre-calculus in high school. Moreover, I was forced to take an art class where I learned to interpret pieces of historically Christian art. Throughout the entirety of these courses, I wondered why I was taking them as a political science major. That lack of reasonable application to my education in political science caused me to care little for my overall performance in these classes. Subsequently, my grades in these classes displayed that low effort, lowering my overall grade average. At graduation, the difference between my major GPA and cumulative GPA were significantly different as a result of the general education requirement courses. This was not solely my experience. Many of my fellow students experienced a similar phenomenon. It is almost like students will study more for the major they selected rather than forced courses on matters that do not relate to their interest. Higher education has seemingly not realized this simple idea yet because they continue to propagate these nonsensical requirements. Throughout my college experience, as I was forced to take courses that had nothing even remotely to do with my college major, I kept asking myself the point of it all. Some of these courses were interesting, but why were they being forced on a political science major? Moreover, these are subjects I could have learned online for free, which is a problem for someone like me who does not like to waste money.

Why are some universities providing courses on Harry Potter, the science of superheroes, or UFOs in American society? These nonsensical courses are usually general education requirement options. In my personal experience, I was forced to take an English course with a barely scholastic outlook. It was a basic English class on writing and argument formation, but the theme of the entire class was based on Feminism in early American literature. Other students I knew were taking courses themed on Harry Potter or satire where they would watch late night shows, discussing the strength of comedian John Oliver's arguments. Though these courses are not the most ridiculous examples of classes that waste time, they demonstrate how the university is slowly degenerating from a prestigious academic institution into a conglomeration of nitwits who do not actually seek education but rather accreditation.

Who benefits from this type of flawed system? Certainly, it is not most graduates as their employment opportunities are so dismal following their four years in higher learning. It is instead the complex of administrators, business, and government that prey on the students entering who think they will get benefits on the other side. I only gained one benefit from my entire time in university: it allowed me to go to law school where an undergraduate degree is required. But most students are expecting return immediately following graduation and want employment in their specific field of study. Sadly, this is not generally the case anymore.

What is this "college experience" that many use as a reason to attend college, and why is that experience increasingly tied to partying or social connections instead of education? This experience was largely absent for me in my time at university because I isolated myself from the idea of partying and making friends. The main reason why I attended university was to acquire education. I wanted to finely tune the ability to read, write, and speak. And, when I discovered that what I thought was the purpose of higher education, namely, to purely gain education, was a thing of the past now replaced by making connections and gaining accreditation, I was thoroughly upset. I was discontent with the system that portrayed itself as an institute for education, but it was something else. It was false advertising at its worst.

How has the recent COVID crisis pointed out that education is not strictly bestowed by colleges and universities and that the higher education system is on the way out? The movement to an online format for most courses in higher education during this time period will be a major game changer. More students will begin to question why they are paying thousands of dollars for an education that can be easily provided online with more convenience. The crisis has illuminated the already present flaws in the system from the lack of utilizing technology to the exorbitant price of the four-year degree. Personally, I did not see any significant difference between the in-person courses compared to the online format. In fact, I believe the change was a major improvement to the class experience because the lectures were recorded to which I could watch them multiple times to reinforce the information. I gained more understanding of the information because I was able to watch the course material in the comfort of my apartment, unbothered by any other distractions that generally occur in the classroom. It is a better system of learning where technology made it possible, but higher education is too slow to change due to bureaucratic politics and massive amounts of money trading hands.

What are the historical roots of college, and what has led to the massive societal stigmas pressuring students to attend colleges? There is a major pressure that high school students feel to attend higher education. Students feel a major stigma surrounding those who do not attend university. The thinking goes that if they do not attend, then they will be viewed as a failure. This stigma has historical roots, and I have personally felt this pressure in deciding to attend university. Many others like me, regardless of their particular skills set, have been influenced by this stigma, too.

Higher education is not for everyone, so what are other options for motivated and smart people who have no interest in attending college? There are plenty of options, and high school students need to take a long and hard look at the different opportunities that are outside of the focus of higher learning.

For those who are going to attend university, there are still major problems with the system, so it is vital to get through it as soon as possible. How did I manage to graduate in two years, or half the time allotted to most students attending a four-year Bachelor of Arts program? No, I did not defraud my university nor was there a program specifically designed for people wanting to graduate in half the time. I went into higher education with a plan; I outlined what I would do and how I would progress. My philosophy before entering was that poor planning creates poor performance, and this should be the motto for those going through the admissions process during high school. More so, they should carry this mentality all the way from admissions throughout the rest of their life.

With all these problems of the higher education system, what are the implications for a system that is failing to produce positive outcomes for so many young adults? The future looks uncertain for those aspiring to gain an education in this system. However, just because the future of the higher education system looks bleak, it does not mean that the coming generations' outcomes will be subsequently desolate. As the system begins to deteriorate, society will begin to evolve into a new normal.

This does not mean I am anti-education. Quite the contrary, in fact, I love education. Reading and learning about various subjects are major passions of mine. The impetus for writing this book was not only my personal discontent with the current higher education establishment but also hearing the stories of other students who are under crippling debt with nothing to show for it. My problem is with a system that overcharges for a degree and does not provide economic benefit to most graduates. Throughout the rest of this book, the questions outlined here will be investigated with more detail and examined through the lens of my college experience. I will offer several ways to improve the higher education system, as well as highlighting other issues plaguing the system and giving way to navigate the system with efficiency. The goal is not to eradicate universities even though that might be the coming future. Rather, it is limited to reforming specific aspects of the system, so it can get back on track for the benefit of future students, their families, and the country.

INTRO TO FAILURE

Part One

———————

Introduction

Chapter I

The Problem that Illuminated Parallel Flaws

"What can be added to the happiness of a man who is in health, out of debt, and has a clear conscience?"—Adam Smith

As of 2020, there are a staggering 45 million people in the United States who finance student loans with a collective amount owed of 1.6 trillion dollars. Apart from mortgages, this astronomically large number is more than all forms of debt including credit cards.[1] This ballooning debt of student loans is at the forefront of many of the discussions regarding the failures of the U.S. higher education system. This single problem has led many to begin investigating more complex issues that permeate the system. While these subsequent problems are fully considered in the main body of this book, the dilemma must be addressed for both its importance and consequential effects.

Why are the debt burdens so high as compared to fifty years ago? In the past, almost no one would question the value of a college degree. However, value of the degree has plummeted, and many point to the student loan debt as proof. The staggering amount of debt is difficult to visualize. The government talks about millions, billions, and trillions of dollars all the time in relation to spending, but most people do not fully realize how much money is being thrown around. If you were to stack one-hundred-dollar bills vertically, one on top of another, one trillion times, it would extend 631 miles. That is beyond the International Space Station, which is only at 248 miles high.[2] Because this problem is the largest, on paper and in reality, it has gained the most attention in the media. Increasingly, people recognize that there is a massive amount of student debt, but they postulate that either nothing can be done, or, more radically, they propose the government should pay all the student debt load.

At this same time of increasing student debt, more students are deciding to go to college. They are signing up for thousands of dollars in debt without a game plan to pay it off or the guarantee of solid employment following graduation. Moreover, it is worthwhile to note that this student debt is not dischargeable in bankruptcy. Therefore, student debt will be with you for life until you pay it off. As tuition continues to rise, the burden to pay off the loans has increased without a subsequent increase in the pay of graduates. The pay for college graduates, in fact, has decreased overall within the past twenty years. This creates a massive problem for students once they graduate, who will struggle to pay the loans back. Further, this debt has real world effects regarding overall societal norms. This is causing major social backlash where graduates with major student loans have put off the purchase of homes, delayed getting married, or postponed having children.[3]

Besides the social determinant of graduates struggling to take financial risk and prolonging aspects of adulthood, there are real damages to the individual, too. People have increased rates of depression and anxiety as a result of the massive debt load, they must pay back with horrible interest rates. So, it is justifiable why people want to understand why tuition is so high and where that money is going. The answer is partly explained by the monetary funds that universities maintain called endowments. Shockingly, the endowments for some universities are enormous. The endowment of Harvard, for example, is approximately 40 billion dollars,[4] which would be enough to put it squarely between Latvia and Bahrain in GDP rankings of countries.[5] The point of endowments is to generally keep the university alive for generations. These funds are invested in private and public equities and several huge funds.[6] However, universities, combining it with student tuition and public donations, use only a small amount of the endowment to pay off the expenses of the fiscal year. Most of the money they bring in from the endowment is used for scholarships, financial aid, and professorships, but they only use a tiny amount from the overall endowment to aid students and for the upkeep of the university itself. They essentially hoard the funds for the university, so the university itself is guaranteed to survive for the long run.

By no means would I argue that universities should use all their endowments to cut student costs because, for institutional and longevity purposes, it is a wise system to which it almost guarantees the university's survival. But, when the endowment of a university is larger than multiple countries in the world, there is something inherently inappropriate about such a system that sets up students for debt while they continue to keep their billions. Something is

3

going to have to change if America wants to slow or end the debt crisis of student loans. Colleges and universities are either going to have to lower tuition via pulling more from the endowment or cut the overhead administration cost that has been a major cause in the rising tuition rates. Pulling in more money from the endowment would be only a temporary solution to the problem of increased tuition rates, as there is only so much money in that pool. Usually, the funds in the endowment are tied into other assets classes that would not easily be transferred over to covering university expenses. Practically, universities will have to radically cut costs, especially the costs that add nothing to the benefit of the diploma. The key is to decrease the administration costs since this is the largest growing expense of universities. These institutions spend copious amounts of money on their presidents and senior administrators, and they continue to hire more and more low-level administrators, which increases the overhead.

This is the most significant part of increased tuition rates called "administrative bloat."[7] Senior administrators and school presidents, as noted earlier, make hundreds of thousands of dollars, and there has been an overall increase in hiring and allocation of funds to administrators and advisors. For example, in the early 1980s, the administrative spending was only about $13 billion of the spending within higher education but has risen significantly to about $122 billion. Universities need to cut the fat. They need to regain fiscal discipline and only spend on what is vital to the maintenance of the university and the overall benefit of the degree conferred. They need to stop spending money on things like student success administrators, senior coordinators, or health promotion specialists. Cut administrative spending by a considerable percentage, in other words. In the short term, it might decrease the number of students who want to attend, but the subsequent decrease in tuition that would accompany the cutting of the administrative fat will attract many more students, raising the overall revenue to the university back to normal. Cutting administration costs will lead to better professors and increased capacity for more students within the university. The universities are wasting this money from the students by funneling it into the administration instead of providing for a better education that leads to a better degree.

Furthermore, colleges and universities are shelling out millions in order to attract prospective students to their schools. They build better buildings, maintain superfluous facilities, and continue hiring more administrators in the aim of attracting new cash cows in the form of gullible students. Multiple universities now have rock-climbing walls as a selling point for prospective students, and some universities have even more luxuries, like lazy river pools or game rooms with pool tables and video games. These are nonessentials when considering a university's goal of pursuing an education. Moreover, students do not realize that they are paying for these things in their tuition, but, eventually, they will have to pay for these luxuries they enjoyed in college through their debt burden.

Another tangential cause of the massive amount of student debt is the decrease in state funding for these institutions, despite the rise in the number of students who are attending. Correspondingly, the university makes up for this lack of government funding by raising tuition rates for students. Subsidizing education is a benefit to society, but only to the degree that it is financially viable. It would be both impractical and unethical to argue for completely free universities, but the idea of more government subsidization for a reasonable priced degree is beneficial. However, I would only advocate increasing the government spending for universities for those institutions that accurately demonstrate that they have cut the inefficiencies of bloated administration. So, if the government does increase its spending on higher education, it will be on things that benefit the society instead of the bloated administration costs that are passed onto the students and the taxpayer.

The argument that university should be free is gaining popularity among many in America, particularly with those who hold the most amount of debt and would gain the most from such a policy change. This argument for free education is based on the idea that an education is a human right. This argument with its explanation of the problem and solution are overly simplistic and erroneous. The government cancelling all current student loans raises a moral question over the fairness to individuals who have worked hard to pay off their student loan debt. The government would be incentivizing the idea that people should not pay their debt because the government might come along and cancel all of it. The government paying for things they declare to be rights is a slippery slope when it comes to fiscal responsibility. Moreover, the government does not make rights; human rights are inherent and endowed through their Creator. Government simply enumerates such rights. With arguments like cancelling student debt because education is a supposed right, this delineation is sometimes forgotten. It would be unethical for the government to cheat the individual who honestly and previously paid off their debt. Also, how is it fair for the taxpayer to completely subsidize another person's voluntary decision to attend a university? Why should someone lose their money if they did not want to attend themselves and instead became a vocational worker?

Declaring something a right does not make it free. Americans possess the right to bear arms, but guns are not free. This logic pointedly applies to the debate on healthcare as some people argue that the service is a human right, so it should be free. However, these people do not address the way in which they would be able to pay for the massive public cost to the taxpayer. And, the argument is basically moot because information and education is generally already free in the modern era as the internet has equalized opportunity to gain education for those who want to learn.

At the turn of the century, the birth of the internet meant the growth of access to information. Websites like Encyclopedia Britannica and others maintain a vast abundance of knowledge on almost any topic one can imagine. This is another reason people are questioning the purpose of university. Universities are now providing credentials to the future employers of students rather than bequeathing an actual education. Because the system is not the only way people can become educated, many are seriously questioning the reason for the institutions in the first place. This dichotomy between the university as an educational institution or one simply to manufacture credentials for its customers is at the forefront of the individual's cost-benefit analysis of college.

Besides the elimination of administrative bloat, there

are other solutions to the problem of the student debt crisis. The most apparent solution is to simply not attend university. As the supply of people who attend increases, the employment demand for the graduate's decreases, producing the current economic conditions where graduates cannot find employment. Because there are so many college graduates, the employment prospects are significantly lower than they were a few decades ago. Lowering the number of college graduates will allow for better employment options as there are more opportunities for those who graduate. Moreover, if there were less people going into college then they might head into skilled positions to help the skills gap. There are not enough people for certain skills and vocational jobs. The skills gap has accounted for about 6.5 million unfilled jobs in 2018. The problem keeps growing because the baby-boomer generation is retiring and leaving skilled jobs, and the younger generations are unwilling to fill these positions. The increase in young people going to college rather than learning specific skills that enable them to take on specific jobs is widening the gap.[8] One of the solutions to bring down the student loan debt is to increase the amount of people going into skilled careers rather than spending time in college. Apprenticeships might be a valuable tool in this process where the connection between technical school and employers can be utilized to close the skills gap. The utilization of funding and incentives by the government to encourage the youth to gain skills for an increasingly technologically centered world outside of the university system is vital to helping the overall economy and the student debt crisis.

For those that decide to attend college or who have already attended and accepted the financial risk of the debt, a possible solution is to have an incentive for employers to make their employees pay off their debt by reserving a certain amount of their income to pay the loans. The process would be like social security or other employer-provided insurance. Although it is not the employer's duty to do this because those who take out the loans should be responsible enough to pay them back. For it was the borrower's decision to take the risk of getting the loan for college, and it is the duty of the person who took the loan to repay it. Generally, employers will only do this if there is some economic incentive to do this, so they could offer this type of program to make small payments on the loans as an incentive for hiring applicants. The employers could either take money out of the employee's overall paycheck or pay the employee slightly more, using that slight raise to pay for their loans. As the debt crisis grows, it will become more lucrative as it might bring companies better applicants. For example, the Bloomberg campaign in the 2020 Democratic primary race was offering such incentives for getting better applicants. Further, many rural hospitals do such programs for students exiting medical school. Similarly, the government has an incentive like this called the Public Service Loan Forgiveness Plan in which one serves in public service for some period. At the end of this period of service to the government, the person's debt is forgiven. However, this is a long time to pay off loans, so it is not applicable to everyone who holds student loan debt.

Among college graduates, there is a lack of adequate financial understanding when it comes to paying off loans. The federal government, who seemingly gives out loans to everyone with a pulse, tries to combat this through the Federal Student Aid website, trying to implement educational tools to help people understand what they are doing. However, the people signing up for the financial burdens are usually high schoolers who do not know anything about loans. Many of these young people are being set up to live under debt, and they usually do not have the emotional or financial control or understanding on how they will begin to pay off their loans in an efficient way.

The overall student loan debt burden is growing at an estimated rate of 7% each year, and it will soon be unmanageable if it continues in this manner. It will be around approximately 3 trillion by the end of the decade.[9] There needs to be sweeping changes within the society regarding the financial responsibility. Moreover, there needs to be an efficient effort by the government, employers, and universities to overcome this challenge or else it will continue to get worse. The period at which people are most likely to take entrepreneurial risks is at the age where most college students graduate. Graduates, however, are not going to take these risks if they are burdened with debt. Loans are good for those that will benefit from them in the long run, and they provide an opportunity for those who do not already have the liquid capital to attend university. Loans given to graduates allow them to become doctors and lawyers, for example. They give people the opportunity to pursue their natural talents. But loans are not good for everyone, and the government is treating it like they are appropriate for everyone who graduates high school. This problem will be one of the most considerable controversies that this generation will have to address, and it will be one in which has deep societal and economic impact if left unchecked.

Chapter II

The University in the Modern World

"Education is the passport to the future, for tomorrow belongs to those who prepare for it today"—Malcolm X

What is a university? Fundamentally, a college or university is an archive of human experience and knowledge along with the essential pursuit to expand that sphere of wisdom. Over the past thirty years, this cornerstone truth about the nature of universities has been moving outside the basic model of higher education. More of the foundations of the universities are moving online, which is now the largest repository of human experience, an enormous catalogue for anyone who has an internet connection. Before the creation of the internet, a solid education was difficult to come by, and it seemed like higher learning was only a luxury of the rich and powerful. But, the freedom of information via the internet available to ordinary people has led the creation of equal educational opportunity to those who seek to progress in the world. The modern university still has some power in that it offers accreditation, but this fact is becoming less valuable as students consider whether it is worth taking on more ruinous debt, starting to look elsewhere for this accreditation. The bloating of salaries and expenses to this massive bureaucracy mean university administrations have essentially taken the future earning power of students and created a generation of debt-holding graduates.

The movement out of universities has grown exponentially with sites like YouTube, where lectures can be uploaded with ease to a wide audience who are actively engaged in the pure pursuit of information. These lecture videos do not have high production quality, but the viewers are not there for that. They are watching because they thirst for information that is not costing them tens of thousands of thousands of dollars and is provided in a convenient manner. This is as influential as the creation of the printing press by Gutenberg in the 15th century, and the effects of the internet are not even realized yet in the modern era. The expanse of human history is enormous; the creation of the internet is a relatively sudden concept which will have major implications for future generations. I believe that it will cause the movement of the classical university system of higher education into an online or blended version to which certain accreditation models could qualify individuals for employment after taking a series of examinations.

Modern universities have been criticized for a lack of true free speech on campuses, the indoctrination of a postmodernist view of the world, and overabundance of politically correct safe spaces. Besides the science, technology, engineering, and math disciplines, which maintain their focus on pure certainties of nature, it has come to a tipping point in which the classical repository of information that universities once were are now becoming so biased toward the postmodern worldview that people are looking toward other places to gain knowledge, like the internet. The modern university will soon become superfluous as more and more of the information they are teaching appears on the internet. Besides accreditation, whose value is also decreasing, the product the higher education system is providing to students is worth almost nothing.

This is the birth of a new era in thinking for all of humanity. The internet has radically changed the ability to disseminate information, and the future of higher education will be on the internet. Now, there are exceptions to this in that a professional school must have some degree of contact and in-person communications for things like labs. But, the majority of undergraduate, and even some professional schools, are becoming expendable as more information from these institutions arise on the internet. With certain accreditation tests or some types of examinations to which only let a minority of takers pass, there is an accreditation that is valuable for providing employers information on whether the applicant is qualified for the position. This type of system would sidestep the universities and may eventually be their downfall. This entire argument might be a case of the old saying: "Don't throw the baby out with the bathwater." However, the baby in this example is disappearing. The entire bathtub is slowly turning into nothing but bath water. As the baby disappears, it might be time to finally throw out the bathwater entirely, and the COVID crisis will be the final nail in the coffin of modern higher education. But, how did the university system become what it is today?

Chapter III

Historical Roots of University

"We are not makers of history. We are made by history."
—Martin Luther King Jr.

A s general American history begins with the colonies, so, too, does the story of higher education in the United States. The beginning of this system was founded with the distinct purpose of producing educated individuals with a religious outlook. Certain colleges were founded to produce graduates assigned to specific denominations who would subsequently be the teachers and leaders of those parishes. Harvard, for example, the oldest college in America, was established to train clergy for Protestant congregations. William and Mary, the second oldest college, maintained a disposition to advance the ambitions and education of the leadership in the Church of England. In the coming centuries, as more people immigrated to North America, Catholic colleges developed within major cities where these immigrant populations substantially increased. As the population of the south increased with agricultural advancements of cash crops like king cotton, Baptist colleges began sprouting up because more of their members resided in this area of the country.[10]

Besides the aspiration to provide education to those

who would preach the word of God, a large part of colleges was the pure fascination of information for the sake of pursuing knowledge and spreading it to all people. In the early years of the universities in the colonies, this included Native American, although these institutions largely excluded women, pushing them to all-female institutions. The early colleges were like common goods where the community would support the institution through voluntary contribution for the pursuit to educate their future leaders. The curriculum focused on theology and languages, especially Latin because of its religious significance to Christianity, even though it was a dead language. The teaching was extremely strict, for example, corporal punishment was administered at Harvard until 1734. The teaching was very academically rigorous, and this extraordinarily high degree of disciplined scholarship provided major and influential statesmen and enlightenment scholars who were instrumental in the subsequent revolution that transpired. The colleges were proximate causes of the revolutions, supplying the leadership of the movement through their teaching of enlightenment principles. It is even argued that these graduates of the colonial colleges expedited the revolution by several decades as they propagated the message that led to revolution.[11]

Though its initial role was regulated to education and the pursuit of knowledge in the realms of moral and religious issues, the colonial colleges began to shift their focus of study to promote more secular views. The community already maintained a deep relationship and adherence to religion, so the universities began to explore the ideas of the enlightenment period, like humanist philosophy and other political theories. In the period leading directly up to the

American Revolution, colleges began to take on more significant issues in the political realm, applying the principles of the enlightenment and the new political theories they learned in university. The greater emphasis on enlightenment and liberal principles influenced the coming revolution and caused conflicts with the English Crown. Through the pre-revolutionary education of these schools, a vast majority of students became ardent patriots and maintained leadership roles during the uprising against the British Crown. As many as five of every six graduates in America in 1776 supported the movement for independence. Every colonial college became a stronghold for Whig ideology, with the notable exception of the Tory-leaning King's College, renamed Columbia College after the American Revolution. Student activism was an extensive part of the collegiate relationship with the early American community and the college experience.[12] One of the founding principles of these institutions was to produce community leaders. The idea that these early colleges were "ivory towers" in which only the elite and rich were able to attend is a misconception. The colleges were active revolutionist centers that were integral to the political and social structures within each state.[13]

Colleges maintained their central role in the community for the next century. The college experience began to shift during this time period with instruction becoming even more strict, especially for men, who were subject to almost military-style training. This quasi-military indoctrination would become a key part of the American Civil War, both the Union and Confederate forces used colleges and the graduates themselves to achieve tactical advantages. West Point Military Academy is one example of an institution providing leadership training, as other colleges and universities had done during the revolution. Moreover, the colleges themselves, including the buildings, beds, and facilities, were used as barracks for soldiers, among other strategic battlefield benefits.[14]

After the Civil War, most notably in the South, the loss of faculty, students, income, and buildings, did not hamper college's ability to play a major role in rebuilding, especially in parts that were demolished by Sherman's march to the sea. The war was over, and universities needed to rebuild their communities and return to educating the public. Confederate soldiers entered the administration of southern colleges with practical experience of leading they had gained from the war. The southern colleges, such as the University of North Carolina, South Carolina College, and the University of Mississippi, now placed their focus on the sciences as opposed to a more military style of teaching and the dogma of Christianity. These southern colleges, however, would teach a history of the Confederacy strikingly different than one taught in the northern universities. They would begin to argue that the South was defending federalism and states' rights rather than racist slavery.[15] Nonetheless, Black colleges and universities began to spread throughout the nation, especially in the South, as many newly freed slaves were eager to become educated. However, there was still major discrimination in the South, especially following the end of Reconstruction in 1877, and the Freedmen's Bureau helped fund these schools. Institutions like Howard University, Atlanta University, and Booker T. Washington's Tuskegee institute provided a place for newly freed slaves to become educated. This would provide what W.E.B. Du Bois referred to as the "talented tenth" in the leadership of the Black community.[16] Discrimination from most universities following 1877 would lead the African American community into the these ancillary institutions, and this would be the case until the American Civil Rights movement of the mid-20th century opened up more universities to be inclusive. There are still remnants of the Reconstruction era on many southern campuses. For example, the University of South Carolina denotes the occupation by Northern troops with a sign just outside the Thomas Cooper library.

Universities continued to play a key role in propagating upward mobility and a great education for graduates far after the Civil War, and they would mold many of the country's future leaders both on the state and federal level. Colleges and universities began to flourish and gain momentum during the 1920s, a time when the country and its economy were growing at an extremely fast rate. But in 1929 the stock market crashed, leading to the Great Depression. Generally, the depression did not significantly affect colleges until it was at its height. Unlike the 2008 financial crisis, the youth did not run to college in order to stay off unemployment and just hide from adulthood. Rather, those who went to university during the Great Depression pursued degrees tailored to the dynamic economy. These students were smart and looked ahead, desiring to have a degree applicable to specific employment after graduation. Despite the funding for colleges and universities beginning to dry up as states were cutting their fiscal budgets, they were still able to provide a valuable degree for incoming students during this time of economic hardship.[17] Eventually, the federal government was able to reduce the financial burden of the universities like it did in 2008, but one of the major keys to the rebound of universities, and the nation as a whole, was the Second World War.

The Second World War presented a great opportunity for colleges and universities as the U.S. Armed Forces required an adequate education for officers and senior leadership, not to mention the need it created to develop new and improved machines and devices to support the war effort. At the end of 1942, there were more than three thousand armed forces personnel attending classes at Harvard.[18] The war caused a shift in higher education, forcing schools to come up with a more flexible curriculum to better serve the needs of the war effort, like a renaissance education. With this type of education, officers would be able to apply historical approaches to problems while also knowing the scientific aspects of important factors in war, so different topics would come together for the benefit of the soldier to survive and find innovative solutions to problems. Understanding the science behind weapons and the math of projectiles along with historical lessons of world history would determine gameplans on attacking the enemy. Moreover, the opportunities for women in the nation skyrocketed, as they were needed to make up for huge gaps in the workforce. Education was a vital part of this process.[19] Therefore, women were able to acquire more education than they ever had in the past, leading to profound consequences after the war, when women began arguing for inclusion in these institutions. The homecoming of troops from abroad, who now were able to gain education at the government's expense, meant a massive influx of incoming students into universities. The GI Bill, officially called the Servicemen's Readjustment Act of 1944, provided a free education as a reward for service to the country. This act set a precedent that would continue to this day of the government providing education to their servicemen. It was a major development of the idea that college was not necessarily a public good, but rather it was an economic advantage to an individual that would propagate one's career.[20] The war truly increased the size and the scope of higher education to one unmatched in any other industry or profession. The government began to funnel money to colleges and universities during and, especially, after the war, creating many aspects of the modern university system.

Since the 1950s, the population in the United States has become increasingly more educated than past generations as more veterans attend college. Moreover, increased funding from the federal government perpetuates the higher education system, as more and more money means better facilities and other resources. This was especially true in times like the Vietnam War, where the universities were gaining in popularity because men would get a deferment from the draft if they attended college.[21] The Cold War with its many proxy wars, the arms race, and the space race gave Congress the incentive to pass legislation for loans and other types of grants that would inflate the number of applicants and students. This was meant to provide for a more educated citizenry that would be able to compete with the Soviet Union. During times of a financial crisis, like in 2008, colleges saw a rise in attendance as people tried to forestall the struggles of finding a job. The rise in the student population within higher education has disproportionately affected public institutions, which have, over time, increased their student body more compared to private universities. Nonetheless, both have increased steadily over the past fifty years from around a total of six million students combined in 1965 to close to twenty million today.[22]

Currently, there are a whopping 5,300 colleges and universities in the United States.[23] Several issues plaguing higher education have their roots in historical trends and events, even if not every problem with the modern university can be traced to a single watershed moment. Regardless, understanding how the higher education system was established is critical in understanding how universities became what they are today and finding the solutions to its problems. For example, the current student loan crisis has its roots in the Cold War goal of education. The idea of providing loans to almost every high school graduate was established on the idea that we must beat the communists by having a supremely educated populus. Therefore, the American society must provide the opportunity for higher education to all high school graduates regardless of skill set. Many of the central flaws of the university system are modern problems that pervade the pursuit of education, with some having their roots in historical trends. Both the modern problems and more complicated historical problems will be discussed in further detail.

Chapter IV

Societal Stigma Regarding College Attendance

"Our individual lives cannot, generally, be works of art unless the social order is also."—Charles Cooley

Go to college or else. This simple yet profound idea regarding the future success of people in the real world pervades an increasing number of high schools in America. Teenagers are told that without a college education they will not be successful in their lives. College will be the ticket to prosperity or, at least, an upper-middle class lifestyle. It will be the start to a happy and a productive life with financial security and a good job. These are the myths of the stigma, propagated by high schools, parents, and students.

Some high schools only have college fairs instead of job fairs. Further, there is a system of funneling students into higher education through academic advisors, who pressure attendance to these colleges and universities. The parents, regardless of their background, will also maintain the social esteem of a college degree, as they want their kids to be a success. They buy into the false narrative that a university education is the key to success, believing that their child will not be productive or successful in life without attaining that very expensive piece of paper called a diploma. Every parent wants the best for their children, so they inevitably advocate the prospect of attending college because that is what they think is the best. They cosign on loans and sometimes encourage their children to attend the best name-brand university possible, regardless of price.

High school students are encouraged to participate in extracurricular activities for the purpose of listing them on their college application's resume. Students are told that being smart is not enough, and activities will make them "well-rounded." Advanced Placement and International Baccalaureate courses maintain a strong disposition for reinforcing the social pressure of attending college. These companies operate on the assumption that students will utilize their accreditation tests for college credit, so they have a financial incentive to pressure students into colleges. If most high school students decided to not attend university, the business model of AP and IB classes would essentially fail. Early on in high school, students are introduced to standardized tests, like the PSAT, SAT, and the ACT. These tests are a key part of most college applications, and students are pressured to succeed on these tests. Teachers, parents, and students emphasize the importance of these tests because they assume that college is the ideal path to success following high school, and these tests are necessary for that pursuit. Although some university systems, such as the University of California system, are beginning to abandon standardized tests, they are still widely used in the admissions process and are a part of a system that pressures students to attend college.[24] The movement away from these tests has both positive and negative consequences. On the one hand, they will lower pressure on students to perform well on the standardized tests, but, on the other hand, universities will move to base their decision on other aspects of the individual, like race, class, and gender. The inconsistency of grades across high schools is a problem for university admissions, solved by standardized test taking. So, the use of these tests is important to the overall admissions process, but they should not be introduced to freshmen in high school because it presumes that they will attend university. Presuming that a high school student will attend college makes it seem like college is the only pathway. Introducing these tests so early on in high school does not give students time to consider other options in vocational or technological fields that are outside of the higher education system.

High schoolers do not have all the information to make decisions that will significantly outline the rest of their life without the guidance of adults within their community, and when there is a pervading stigma for *not* attending college, students think there is no other option. They think they will fail in life if they do not attend college. After going through all these activities from standardized testing to engaging in resume-boosting extracurriculars, there is a sunk-cost fallacy that occurs with students. Unconsciously, these high school students have put so much time, effort, and money into what seems like requirements for college that they might as well attend as to not lose all that hard work already completed. They were not given any other options or activities that would lead them to possibilities other than college. The process makes a positive feedback loop as these same high school graduates enter college, graduate, and become those who reinforce the stigma of not attending a four-year program.

They feel a need to justify their decision to get a degree.

With all these pressures, it is not difficult to see why so many high schoolers in America feel it is necessary to attend a college or university. The binary choice presented to them is to either succeed or to fail, to go to college or to founder through life. Most high schoolers, administrators, and parents across the country frown upon being a vocational artist or a person with other trade skills, not within the scope of academia. High schoolers will continue to see it as their only option to get ahead, and this process will continue to inflate the number of students who attend colleges and universities, exacerbating the student loan crisis and enlarging the skills gap in the United States. There fundamentally needs to be more options for student's post-high school graduation without the social stigma. Further, the assumption that they will fail in life without a college degree needs to be eradicated. Multiple factors lead people to success in life, everything from hard work and dedication to IQ and talent.

Along with hundreds of thousands of other students, I was brainwashed with this same thinking. Essentially, I maintained the mentality in high school that I would be a failure without the piece of paper celebrating a college education. No other options besides college were presented to me at the time. Moreover, students looked down upon those who decided not to attend college or decided to attend a community college, even though it was only one or two of them in my class who chose not to attend a four-year university. Witnessing this stigma regarding college persuaded me and many more students to take the path of college. There are exceptions to this generality in that the stigma is not the same across all high schools. Schools in more industrial areas will usually not experience the stigma as much while high income areas will experience it more. But, overall, the stigma of not attending higher education is a growing trend.

I had an experience during high school that illustrates the pressure on high schoolers to attend university. During my sophomore year, I became a more academically-inclined student, performing extremely well in all my classes. There were many reasons for this, but too many to explain and far too complex psychologically. Nonetheless, I began to achieve straight As in all my courses regardless of the material. I thought this was enough for any college to accept me, based on the assumption that college is the next step in education. After all, were not these institutions solely devoted to the pursuit of that education and its expansion? However, one morning, I was at my locker, preparing for the day and about to head for the library. The teacher who led the Model UN team, and who was my teacher for freshman year history, came up to me to ask how I was doing and about my grades. He asked if I was participating in any extracurriculars. At that time, I merely enjoyed grappling with and understanding the concepts learned in class. In addition, I was concerned with learning new things outside the classroom via documentaries and reading books. So, when I said I was not in any extracurriculars, he told me to join some because colleges want "well-rounded candidates."

Because I wanted to succeed in life, and the fact that college was presumably the only option, I decided to join the clubs and other activities to improve my odds of college admissions. Although the teacher did this with great compassion, and while I thoroughly enjoyed my time on the team, this was a prime example of the pressure students come

27

under as they go through high school. Teachers and parents begin to encourage students to participate in activities because they are building a resume for college as opposed to activities that might lead them into another career field entirely outside of college, like wood-working or plumbing. Once thought of as activities to explore interests, high school extracurriculars are now becoming something to do for the resume instead of career interest or pure enthusiasm. Activities that were once useful for skilled workers, who did not want to attend university, like wood shop or factory working, are being replaced with art or music. A certain argument for students entering college en masse is that it will make them well-rounded, renaissance people. But what is the point to already require such a character before one goes to college? What can college add to a person who is already a well-rounded person?

Nonetheless, I took this message about extracurriculars to an extreme and joined several organizations solely for the purpose of building my resume for applications. The same mentality applies with the approach to standardized exams in which students spend hours studying for examinations in the hope that a high score will give a boost to their applications. All this even though they do not yet know if college is necessarily the right option for their future. In my experience, I focused most of my summer before senior year of high school going over practice exams of the ACT. I spent days going through the material for the English and math sections along with making plans to strategically approach the reading and science sections. Even though I finally achieved a score of thirty-three, the time could have been better spent researching future career options. Or instead of spending hundreds of hours studying the best approaches to taking a test for college, I could have been using the time to learn new things on my own by reading or watching documentaries. Arguably, I could have learned more in the latter situation than the former. Although studying for the ACT studying could provide students with basic comprehension skills, students are mostly learning how to take the test rather than learning the material topics reflected in the exam. Strategies to taking standardized exams make knowing the material not as important as knowing how to take the test itself. There are patterns in the test that can be learned instead of understanding higher concepts in topics like math, English, reading, and science. The standardized test scores will sometimes help with scholarships, but that is only for those who are going to attend college and that sunk-cost fallacy comes up again after students take exams like these. Standardized tests along with AP credit and CLEP exams are vital tools for some people, but they should not be compelled by the high school system on students who are not inclined to attend university.

There are overarching societal stigmas that strongly persuade high school students to pursue higher education, even though it might not be the most appropriate path for their future. Obviously, the experience of each high schooler is different. Some students do not feel this pressure because of cultural or social differences within their communities, or their high schools maintain an open attitude towards careers outside higher education. The point, though, is that this stigma is becoming increasingly pervasive in high schools, which is proven by the increase in the number of students going straight into college over the past 50 years.

Correspondingly, this stigma creates a positive feedback loop where many jobs now require a four-year degree, even though there is nothing inherently beneficial the degree brings to the table for those specific jobs. Further, high school students want to impress others by the perceived greatness of the college they attend along with making their parents proud by attending that school. Why is there this social stigma that pressures students to go to university? The idea began early in the 20th century when access to information was scarce, and a college education was valuable. That idea of value feeds into the mentality of students, parents, and administrators of the modern era where they think that university education is the best choice for a better life because it essentially guaranteed one in the past. We must let go of the past, and we must clearly see the problems with universities now and evaluate its utility on current, and not past, standards. Parents need to give their children an understanding of the current job market and the reality that it does not provide as much opportunity as it did in the past. Even though this is a problem that is not precisely about the higher education system, it is a vital one to understand since it is where the other problems of the higher education system essentially begin. The problems of higher education in America begin with this societal stigma because it is the propagating force that pressures students to attend university, exacerbating the failures already within the system.

Part Two

The Failures of Modern Higher Education

Chapter V

The Waste of Two Years

"A man who dares to waste one hour of time has not discovered the value of life."—Charles Darwin

Most university programs that require the usual four-year commitment have a core curriculum undertaken in the first two years of studies. This is commonly referred to as general education requirements or "gen-ed." The higher education system purports that these classes are vital to the overall learning of the student. They provide a basis for continued education in higher-level courses and give students background knowledge in subjects helpful to their career and future education.[25] Even if the course has nothing even remotely pertaining to your major, they are nonetheless important to the overall development of the student into a scholar. Courses in basic math, English, and history are foundational to all majors and help students think outside the box and explore new things that were once unfamiliar.

This is the "myth" of general education requirements for college, and it is one of the considerable problems with higher education. It has been leading to an increase in the debt burdens faced by many students as it makes them spend more time learning things that do not apply to their career.

Granted, everyone who enters college will have different backgrounds from high school or work experience, but these required classes are a waste of money and time, especially considering they cost just as much as classes pertaining to majors. At seven universities, one can take classes on the *Harry Potter* novels.[26] I assume these classes are interesting, but would you pay thousands of dollars to take these classes or want to be required to take them? Emphatically, I would not. They are a waste of time and barely provide the foundation for students to continue into under division coursework. Moreover, a student in the university can do these things on their own time, gaining just as much or even more than they would in a class in college. If you are a biochemistry major, would you pay tens of thousands of dollars to learn basic English writing skills when that information is online for free and does not even remotely relate to your major. If you were an English major, would you pay thousands of dollars for chemistry teaching? Again, if given the choice, I would not. However, universities are forcing their students to take such classes at the student's own cost of tuition.

From personal experience, there were classes available to me that related to satire and late-night shows that satisfied the English requirements of the gen-ed curriculum. In addition, I was forced to take a class on Feminism Through Literature in which I was supposed to learn the fundamentals of English and writing, but it did not provide anything of substance for my major. More infuriating was the requirement as a political science major, something which meant little for my future professional career. It is a cash grab for the universities because all students must fulfill these requirements with most students having to take them through the university, providing the system with more tuition dollars and adding to the debt crisis. Another example of this cash grab is universities requiring you to pay tuition for the credits gained through an internship, whether it is paid or unpaid. Like many other aspects of the university system, the general education requirements are time vampires and cost inefficient, becoming worse over the past thirty years as more students enter the system.

The lack of efficiency at the beginning of my higher learning was my motivation for looking into the flaws of college. The exploration began in calculus where nothing I was learning was even tangentially related to my major. Like many other college students enduring this gen-ed experience, I just sat there and kept wondering why I was learning derivatives when I was a Political Science major. It was a complete waste of time that could have been better spent studying Political Science topics, making my degree worth more because of an increased amount of applicable knowledge relevant to my field. At minimum, if universities continue with general education requirements, they should relate to the specific major of the student. Requiring calculus for an English major is ineffective in the goal that universities have for general education requirements as foundational courses. Moreover, some of these courses that might be able to satisfy the requirements are not even related to academia. Students, for example, can take a class on the Strategy of StarCraft at the University of California Berkeley.[27]This is supposedly a top-tier higher education institution designed to produce some of the world's most ground-breaking research. However, these types of electives that do not even relate to academia should not be within the scope of university spending. Furthermore, students should not be forced to take these types of classes just because they are referred to as general education. There are many classes like the one above in several universities, and this hints at the border problem of college seemingly doing everything they can to become pointless.

Many claim that if they were unnecessary, then they would not have stayed in the course curriculum for so many years. However, this reasoning is flawed because there are other reasons that it has stayed in the curriculum like the financial benefits to the university system. The extra tuition gained from the average student is very important in perpetuating the system of higher education, and it is one of the main reasons that it continues to be in place and maintained as a requirement for students. Proponents of the gen-ed system espouse that people do not know what they want to do with their life when they get to college, so the first two years will allow them to gain experience and figure out what they want to do.[28] This is foolish and shortsighted. These advocates are essentially claiming that it is okay to sign up for the massive debt burden of college while having no idea what you are even going to do when you get there. It is okay to switch your major in college, but to come into college with no game plan, trying to figure it out when you get there, is a major problem for students and an utter failure of the higher education system to actually look for what is best for students.

Many students who accept this idea of figuring it out when I get there come into college with the wrong mindset, and they lack the game plan necessary to complete their degree with efficiency. Inevitably, many college students will get caught up in trying to fulfill these requirements and figure out what to do next. Universities prey on students like these. Advisors coax them into taking classes that might have nothing even remotely to do with their majors. Even though I suspect that advisors generally want to help students, they go about it in the wrong way, which contributes to the overall failures of university. Incoming freshmen are being set up to fail in the future if they do not have a solid game plan prior to entering college. Understanding the risks you take by going to college and the ways in which you will return on your investment from that risk before you enter is vital to success during and following college. If you do not know what you are doing before you enter college, it is not wise to go and blindly stomp around in classes without any semblance of focus. Get a job or defer college for a time to gain real world experience to determine your interests so you can go to college with a game plan. This game plan is how you finish higher education quickly and efficiently, and this mindset applies to almost everything in life where prior preparation is key to success.

Generally speaking, in regards to most universities, the general education requirement is about forty to sixty credit hours, which amounts to thousands of dollars in basic education that can be received in alternative forms outside of college.[29] Moreover, the opportunity costs of losing two years could be massive for students majoring in productive STEM fields and who will achieve a high salary immediately following graduation. They might need to know how to effectively write, but if they do not already have minimal writing skills required for college, they should not be in the university in the first place. There are, however, strict and long requirements for each major, which is not what I am criticizing. These requirements are actual building blocks as opposed to the gen-ed requirements that are only tangentially related or completely irrelevant. Also, one could make the argument that internships during those summers during the first two years are important for the overall progression of the career, but those internships can be done during the major courses of the usual third and fourth years. Personally, I completed an internship during the summer that was helpful and graduated early without wasting too much time on the gen-ed requirements. So, both graduating early and interning are not mutually exclusive. There is nothing wrong per se with the course material of gen-eds, but universities are training the students to be academics with a wide spectrum of information, which can be gained for free, instead of creating scholars who are adept in their particular field.[30] There should be a fundamental shift in how universities approach the first two years of their educational structure.

From my personal experience, advisors recommended that I stay longer in college. Why would they do this? I had completed all my requirements and gained the degree for which I sought, so why would they want me to take more classes and explore more? The reason is that people and organizations respond to economic incentive, and the tuition lost to the university was more important than the overall progression of my career. I assume that the advisors acted in good faith, but it was not necessary if the goal of the diploma is to progress your career and enter the field of your choice. Unless your goal is academia itself, the advisors should be there to get students through the degree requirements as fast as possible. But, overall, they need to implement solutions that remedy the waste of time and money that accompany the first two years of universities.

A couple ideas come to mind in solving the problem of this waste of the first two years of most students' college experience. How about just disbanding the courses entirely and making it a requirement for those who enter college to have the requisite knowledge to jump into their foundational courses in a major? Or maybe universities should maintain different costs for different classes as compared to standard credit hour price. For example, a gen-ed class would cost less than the major-related class since they do not confer a postgraduate benefit. Another idea is to make these gen-eds an optional aspect of the college experience, allowing students to head right into the major course work, sink or swim, leaving the decision to do the added work of the gen-eds until later. Or, if they fail going right into the main course work, then they get sent back to the gen-eds. This would be a gradual move away from gen eds in which the high school and the individual have more responsibility before they enter the university. College and universities often accept dual-enrollment work, like AP and IB credit and CLEP exams. These are useful tools for getting ahead, but not everyone has those opportunities, yet are intelligent enough to jump into the major. Making the gen-eds an option for only those that absolutely need or want them would be a significant step in decreasing the waste of the first two years, and it would almost certainly shorten the time students spend in university as a whole, allowing for students to save more time and money.

Chapter VI

Apathy and Low Academic Standards

"Science may have found a cure for most evils; but it has found no remedy for the worst of them all – the apathy of human beings."—Helen Keller

I t is early in the morning, 8:00 a.m. The college campus is bustling with squirrels milling about the grounds while the songbirds cavort. This is the time just before the first class of the day for a select number of students. These students are the bravest of all students because they dare to take such early morning classes, vehemently disliked by most college students. Many students even take different courses with different professors just to simply avoid this time of class meeting, but why are these classes so hated? The simple answer is that it is difficult for students to wake up early. The more protracted analytical answer is that there is a growing trend of apathy among college students regarding the education itself and the process of higher education feeding into the job market. In addition, the academic standards of the universities are faltering, thus allowing for a negative feedback loop of indifference that continues to grow on college campuses.

INTRO TO FAILURE

I would be sitting in class paying attention to the professor, attempting to understand the concepts and engage in discussion, while a vast number of students were using their phones, watching Netflix on their computers, or sleeping openly in front of the professor. Before and during class, I usually looked around at the students' faces, and I would see an utter lack of commitment and enthusiasm for the class. These students seem annoyed, bored, and fatigued with the class and college. Even more, many of my fellow students would show up significantly late or not even show up at all. How is this behavior preparing students for the real world? Not showing up on a regular basis or being late may cause you to be fired on the spot in the real world. Professors and the universities try to combat this by the institution of absentee limits. For example, if a student is absent for six classes, he or she is deducted a letter grade. But, a lot of professors simply do not have the time to call the attendance role of hundreds of students. Professors might also use I-clickers for attendance with short quizzes at the beginning of the class, but students can easily cheat their way through these by giving their clicker to a friend, even if this is an ethical violation.

Why would someone attend college if they are this bored with the classes and lack the requisite dedication to flourish within the major they chose themselves? The students who seemingly do not care are presumably continuing the same mentality that they had in high school of thinking it does not matter. They have not had much life experience to motivate them to pursue the goal of engaging with the material. There was an eight-year veteran U.S. Air Force airman in one of my history classes and, compared with the rest of the class, he was always squared away. He knew how important college could be if you tried to learn the material instead of slacking off like a growing number of students on campuses. The universities try to infuse life experience into students through work-study positions, study abroad programs, and internship offers, but a lot of college students take their education for granted and subsequently do not care much about the class material.

This is a growing trend on college campuses, even if there still are many hard-working students who actively engage with the material and succeed in the curriculum. Although some of the students are not apathetic, students are not required to work as hard as previous college educated generations. Compared to students of just a few decades ago, college students today spend approximately 50% less time studying their course material.[31] Moreover, a significant amount of the time is spent with their peers, studying in a social setting that is generally not helpful to overall retention of knowledge. Overall, students in modern universities spend only a fifth of their weekly time on academic pursuits—that is combined study, lab, and class time.[32] For someone like me who just exited college, this is not really a surprise. It was obvious that many students did not care about the class as could be seen on their facial expressions during the class itself and their lack of engagement in discussions. Repeatedly, professors would ask questions to the class and receive no answer because students were simply not prepared for class and did not complete the assigned readings. Apathy is not the only reason students are studying less. Some majors require less from students. A communication major will not have as much work as a geophysics major.[33] There is an overall trend that suggests students are not as actively engaged in the course material as they once were and are studying less. Although I am focusing on the humanities and non-STEM related fields, the main trend is growing in all areas of the university. Another aspect that might explain the lack of focus for students is that many in college work part-time jobs to afford the cost of this education. Therefore, they are not able to study as much as their peers.[34] This is unfortunate because economically disadvantaged students cannot engage fully with the material.

Professors are increasingly experiencing the apathy of their students with the new age of technology. Some students come to class without writing utensils or notebook and ask the professor to post the material online. Many students bring laptops, but they do not take notes with them. They instead use them to goof around while the professor is speaking because they can get the information later when it is posted online. The students are becoming helpless, and the professors are on the fence on whether to bow to their sloth or to stand their ground to demand more from their students.[35] Some professors do not implement strict rules in class that would force students to read the sections of the assigned books. These professors are coddling the students in that they do not enforce strong academic standards for their classes. Many of the professors seem not to even care about teaching and do very little to motivate their classes. Many professors are focused on research rather than teaching. Tenure of some professors adds to the indifference, which leads to increased student detachment. Why should students care about engaging with the material if the professor seems to only care about his or her research? There are great professors out there that do an amazing job teaching, but universities need to reorient their focus to higher academic standards and better teaching, so the degree the students gain is worth as much as it costs to obtain.

Another problem is that some professors delegate a considerable amount of grading and the teaching itself to teacher's aides, commonly referred to as TAs. These teachers are vital for helping the professor handle the burden of teaching hundreds of students at a time, but when students come into the university, it is not expected that they will be taught by someone other than the professor. Even though some TAs are great at doing their job at helping students understand the material, they perpetuate the cycle of lower academic standards because they are usually more flexible to the desires of students. Sometimes, a third of a student's credit hours are taught by these TAs, and it is generally not what the students are intending to pay for when they come to university. Universities must focus more on teaching than researching. Also, if the supply of entering freshmen decreased then the professors could maintain smaller classes, making TAs superfluous. Hopefully, as the stigma regarding not attending college decreases, the number of students who attend university will also decrease. Another possibility is the university hiring more professors in place of the administrators, who make up the ever-growing bureaucracy.

I have personally experienced the downhill nature of the academic standards of universities in almost every class I took in my two years at university. I do not think of myself as a model student, but I was always early to each class and attended every time. I engaged with the material and participated in class discussions, but I usually did not do the readings and barely studied outside of class. I never studied for an exam throughout my college experience, and it was a breeze with my major of political science and cognate in history. For example, I walked into my cumulative final exam for Modern German History without studying anything. I did not look over my previous notes; I did not look over the readings. I did not even look over the study guide provided by the professor. However, I got a 98 on the exam. I did not know more than the average student coming into the class, but I was able to get an A with doing just the bare minimum. Overall, I graduated with Latin honors, but I never studied for an exam and barely completed the assigned readings. The academic standards within universities, especially within the humanities, are plummeting, and professors are giving better grades as compared to past generations, which is known as grade inflation.[36] This makes one of the tools used by employers to select candidates worthless, and the overall degree becomes less valued as more people receive the same degree with the same overinflated grade point average.

The usual college student comes into the system being away from parental supervision for the first time, and those who were pressured by their parents to study hard in high school no longer have that influence. The pressure to do well is there, but it only hits the student when they graduate and must get a job and start paying back all the loans they took out. These same college students party and disregard class engagement, trying to slide by with the bare minimum so they can enjoy the college experience. Students are generally coming right out of high school too, so they have not been subjected to harsh realities of the real-world. Thus, many of them maintain a predisposition towards apathy in their academic life, an attitude that will pervade their actions until the reality of adulthood takes control. Students come into college to prolonged infancy, staying off responsibility. The universities are coddling their students by lowering standards in the classrooms, and this perpetuates the apathy. Generally, it is okay for high school students entering college to not have that much real-world experience, but the universities need to prepare students for the real world by encouraging maturity through a strict curriculum.

If a spectator were to go onto a university campus during the time in between classes and look at the students walking around, he or she would see students acting more like drones than human beings. Most people look very upset or tired; they are not talking to other students while they are walking around. In fact, they usually have earbuds in, so they do not have to talk to anyone, especially people handing out flyers or pamphlets. This lack of interaction, even within classrooms where there is almost no conversation between the students before class, is a very real problem. It creates an atmosphere of intellectual isolation instead of a place where students feel free to express different opinions and engage in a group for the pursuit of knowledge. Universities cannot force students to interact with one other nor would it be wise to ban earbuds or things like that, but students need to take it upon themselves to interact with other students to further a teamwork mentality of pursuing knowledge. Encouraging teamwork and conversations among students will allow groups to decipher the complications of any information being learned. In my personal experience, I would almost never go out of my way to engage with classmates on subjects, and I, too, looked like a drone walking around campus with earbuds in, feverishly trying to avoid people trying to talk to me or give me informational pamphlets. In hindsight, this was one of my major regrets of my time in college because working as a team is very beneficial for understanding complex information and solving problems.

Another thing a spectator would see on college campuses is a peculiar style of dressing for class with many students putting little to no effort in their presentation to the outside world. Many students show up to class in pajamas rather than appropriate clothes that make a young person look presentable to a prospective employer. This might just be a personal pet peeve, but I think this mentality of wearing pajamas to class speaks to the apathy of students not caring about how they present themselves. They do not take the responsibility to wake up slightly earlier to put on a pair of pants and a jacket. I see it as a lack of maturity that is presented objectively to the rest of the world. One of the first steps to accepting the responsibility of adulthood is to dress for it. Universities might start to enforce a dress code, which would be a great start to making the immature college student accept responsibility. It might begin to lower the overall apathy of the student body. Many business schools enforce a dress code, where one must wear a suit jacket to class, but I think that this should be applied to the entire university. It will bring back some of the prestige that universities once maintained when students would dress to impress on campus.

There are exceptions to the low academic standards and student apathy, but those exceptions are within a few universities out of the thousands that make up the higher education system. These universities at the top of the top are not necessarily the institutions that I have issues with. Places like Harvard or Yale do a great job in maintaining high academic standards, which lead to lower than average student apathy. Even though they suffer from some of the other major problems like the rest of higher education and have problems with grade inflation, they are still high achieving places where most students are academically challenged. It is these universities at the top that might be worth having students attend, however, these institutions significantly limit one's ability to move through them quickly using AP credits and dual enrollment. These top universities will be the last ones to begin to collapse when the higher education system begins eroding, but they will still modestly degenerate, nonetheless. I commend these institutions for maintaining high academic standards, but that does not excuse them of the other failures that they partake in like wasting the first two years on gen-ed classes and making students into debt slaves. Also, the military academies do an amazing job of screening out apathetic students, and these institutions also maintain very high academic standards, even presenting an exception to the waste of two years because the students of the military academy might need these classes in their military career. Even though the military academies in the country maintain high academic standards and have low student apathy, they have an entirely different set of problems relating to politics and government.

Within the problem of low academic standards and apathy in higher education, there is the related issue of cheating on college campuses. I never cheated on anything during my college experience, achieving my good or bad scores with integrity. However, I heard from friends during college who witnessed cheating on exams in a class. More so, I heard about how students would borrow answers for homework or other assignments as though it was authorized.

Also, they informed me that students would simply look up answers to test questions for online examinations. This would be very easy because the questions with answers were usually on Quizlet, allowing students to make almost perfect scores. My high school had some online exams, but the teachers made the questions so unique that looking the answer up would be almost impossible. However, university professors who have online exams seem too lazy to implement such a policy. A recent study demonstrated that around three quarters of college students admit to cheating during their time in college.[37] Even though the percentage has not changed much over the past few decades, cheating is one of the most abhorrent breakdown of scholarship within higher education. One of the reasons why this is happening is because the academic standards are so low. Students are less inclined to believe that an institution is deserving of their honesty if they do not respect the institution and the degree conferred. Universities need to crack down more harshly on cheating. Colleges need to do more than just make it clear cheating is unauthorized. The professors themselves need to be extraordinarily harsh when it comes to cheating. Moreover, personal responsibility comes into the solution to cheating in that students must confront each other regarding cheating if they see other students doing it. It will help the college community overall, and it will increase the value of the degree if cheating is entirely stomped out of the higher education system.

Universities need to adopt a sink-or-swim mentality. They need to stop coddling their students. They need to implement real world stressors on their students, and they need to adhere to strict academic guidelines in order to have their degree mean something again. University students need to come into higher education with laser focus and radical concern for their pursuit of knowledge. In addition, universities need to increase the difficulty and structure of the classes. Professors must be stricter with students when it comes to doing the assignments and readings. These professors need to focus more on molding the students and infusing the knowledge into them instead of spending most of their time on their research. Student development needs more attention in the modern era where students are graduating with astronomical debt burdens and little to show for it.

Chapter VII

Drinking, Partying, and Illegal Conduct

"It's a great advantage not to drink among hard drinking people."—F. Scott Fitzgerald, The Great Gatsby

Common stereotypes of the college experience frequently paint portraits of naive and careless adolescents partaking in excessive drinking at parties, pre-games, or just weekend hangouts. Many questions whether this stereotype is in fact true. Usually, stereotypes are misleading; they reduce very complex issues to overly simplistic representations of reality. However, there is more truth to this stereotype than one would think, and it is one of the greatest impairments to the higher education system.

Here are the facts: In recent surveys, more than fifty percent of full-time college students between the ages of 18 to 22 consumed alcohol within the past month. Moreover, this survey purports that approximately 36 percent of that same age group participated in binge drinking.[38] Binge drinking is defined as a male consuming 5 or more alcoholic drinks or a female consuming 4 or more alcoholic drinks in under 2 hours. Other national surveys state that the percentage of college students who engage with heavy episodic drinking is approximately 44 percent.[39] The most likely group to binge drink are those below the legal drinking age limit of 21 years old, which is the precise age group of a majority of college students. Those within this specific age group are more likely to engage in binge drinking if they are enrolled in college as compared to those who are not in college.[40] What is even worse is the results of such drinking in which there are approximately 1,400 student deaths, 500,000 injuries, 696,000 assaults, and 97,000 sexual assaults and date rapes, as a result of unintentional alcohol-related causes.[41] Universities are not doing enough to combat the main issue of drinking on campus. They are instead trying more to combat the tangential results of under-age drinking like sexual assaults, poor academic performance, and deaths. There are several reasons college students consume alcohol at an alarming rate, ranging from loneliness or low self-esteem to anxiety or depression. But, the greatest reason that a majority of students drink is due to peer pressure and the overall atmosphere of college in which it is assumed that students engage in such behavior.

Considering my personal experience, I have never drank alcohol and presumably never will for many reasons, but there was an overarching understanding within college that drinking alcohol was a common and even accepted practice. Although colleges and universities purport to maintain a dry campus, in which the student may not have alcohol on the grounds, along with other banned substances, there was generally a lack of supervision regarding the use of prohibited substances. It is easy for the average college student to obtain substances in a bag and transport it into their dorm room. Meanwhile, the resident advisors who oversee these residences are no more than college students themselves. In my personal experience, they did a horrible job at stopping the use of illegal substances within dorms. The resident advisors would even participate with other students in underaged drinking, sometimes even providing the substances for the students in the dorms. Every college is different, and many resident advisors do a wonderful job at policing the dorms for students doing illegal activities, but it is just as easy for those same students to walk to a bar with a fraudulent identification and binge drink with friends. A recent study found that out of a thousand college students, two-thirds of them used fraudulent identification in order to buy alcohol at least once during their time as a student.[42]

Some universities are further reinforcing the drinking culture by allowing the sale of alcohol on campus events like sporting games or concerts. The university justifies this move by claiming the community will benefit, and it will not adversely affect the student body. There are several consequences to this idea, namely, older students above the age of 21 drinking will set a social standard among other students in which it will seem normal to other younger students. It will also signal to students that the university's policy on drinking is becoming more lenient, thus encouraging more students to test the boundaries of the policy and continue drinking while on campus. Further, the idea of having students drink at campus events is counterproductive to multiple university health initiatives that discourage drinking. Therefore, when the university opens the doors to drinking at campus events, they are being hypocritical on their stance toward alcohol. More so, the reopening of alcohol sales will cause a slippery slope in which alcohol sales will permeate into other parts of the university, possibly even dining cafeterias.[43]

One of the things that upset me the most while attending college was the idea that drinking alcohol was just an accepted normal. In fact, I have been to multiple college campuses where the consumption of alcohol by underaged students was a commonality and socially acceptable. Some universities might have less of an issue regarding alcohol consumption by their students, differing slightly on a case-by-case basis. However, the problem writ large is ever present in that a preponderance of college students engages in such detrimental activities. For example, almost all my friends in university had fake identification, so they could go downtown to bars to drink. This could be just the people I associated with in my dorm hall, but as the statistics represent, it is more pronounced than just my anecdotal experience. Traveling to other schools, students also had fake identifications to engage in underaged drinking. Moreover, during my participation in the Reserve Officer Training Corps (ROTC), the safety briefs at the end of labs assumed college students would engage in drinking. Rather than emphatically telling the ROTC cadets to not drink at all because they are underaged, cadre would advise us to not go out alone. This is good advice, but the problem is that they are communicating to the students that it is presumed they will drink, so it might even encourage them to engage in such activities. Also, the issue here is that they are trying to combat the symptoms of excessive drinking rather than confronting the disease itself. My social media accounts were inculcated with pictures of my friend engaging in this type of conduct, and large social media networks like Barstool or Old Row are propagating forces that encourage students to drink in excess. If someone outside the higher education system were engaging in this conduct at the same age they would be described as a deadbeat, but it seems perfectly fine for college students to binge drink. There is a type of elitist double standard within higher education that seems to approve the conduct within the system.

One counter argument is that students will be able to make connections and lifelong memories through drinking. They claim this kind of behavior is fun because it is the only time which you will not have to work and have the stress of adulthood. Essentially, their claim is to prolong youth at the expense of the reality of the real world through the consumption of alcohol. This argument is centrally flawed. Students can make connections with lifelong memories without the use of alcohol. College experience should not be centered around the idea of drinking. Students should find enjoyment in the pursuit of knowledge for that should be the main embodiment of the ethos of university. Another argument I often hear is that some students are above the legal age limit for the consumption of alcohol. However, this is still problematic. Even if these students host parties or drink themselves, they still engage in binge drinking, and if the gathering or party is large enough, they will have limited authority over who drinks at the event. It is fine for those who are over the age limit to drink responsibly off campus, but I still do not recommend it as it impedes the pursuit of education. The problem arises when they drink too much and allow others who are not old enough to participate. It denigrates the entire college experience for those who actively seek to just learn and participate in sober clubs and activities. Furthermore, it degrades the prestige of the degree as employers and outside onlookers view college students as perpetual drinkers.

One of the arguments I hear in relation to halting the drinking and partying atmosphere of college is that it will promote students to go to bars alone. They think that advocating for a halt to drinking on campuses will create a lack of safe drinking education. Their straw man argument purports that if university administrators tell students not to drink, then they will not be able to teach safe practices because it is hypocritical for universities to do so. Universities should make sure students are able to drink safely, like encouraging buddy systems so no one is alone when they drink. The buddy system is a positive aspect that most colleges teach, but it is approaching the problem with the assumption that nothing is going to change, and students will continue to drink. Universities should focus their aims on the heart of the problem instead of the symptoms, trying in every way possible to decrease the amount of drinking on campus and the surrounding areas for those under the legal age. It is fundamentally backwards to passively assume that nothing can be done about the drinking culture on campuses. Solving the consequential effects of the main issue will never fully solve the problem.

Many students and administrators do not want to have this conversation about drinking alcohol on and off campus. Rather they become angry about sexual assault on campus. Many claim that there is even a culture within college campuses that promotes sexual assault. (The people positing these claims are generally on the left of the political spectrum.) I do not buy the claim. I do not believe there is a culture promoting sexual assault. Instead, there is a culture of excessive drinking, which results in more sexual assaults. I would bet my life savings on the correlation that once alcohol is effectively banned on and off campus that the number of sexual assaults would dramatically decrease. The key words here are "effectively banned." Universities have policies in place, but they barely enforce them. They need to get control of the situation.

Some universities do a fantastic job in policing the issue of underaged drinking on and off their campuses. But they need to take a far stricter, hardline approach to the use of alcohol on campus. If a person is caught with alcohol on campus, they should be immediately expelled. There should be randomized dorm checks for the use and possession of alcohol, and there needs to be better security to crack down on the use of fraudulent identifications. Universities should better communicate with the police and surrounding bars to enforce a policy of expelling underaged alcohol users. If students were threatened with expulsion, then there would be a decrease in the use of alcohol on the campus. This needs to be a strict liability offense in which expulsion is mandatory for someone caught drinking underaged. Moreover, those college students providing alcohol to minors should also be expelled. This type of policy should also apply to those caught with using or possessing other types of substances that are banned on campus, like tobacco. There should also be better enforcement in place against the use or possession of drugs. In the past 30 years, the use of marijuana has become a popular phenomenon for students, and universities are too weak to crack down on its use.

Here are some more facts: In 2017, studies stated that 38 percent of full-time college students claimed to have used marijuana within the past year, and a further 21 percent claim to have used it within the past month.[44] This is the highest level in 35 years, and it continues to rise. In 2018, studies displayed a five percent increase to those who have used the illegal substance in the past year. This might be a change in societal standards, as in the early 1990s approximately 75 percent of young adults claimed that the substance was risky, and that number has decreased to about 22 percent.[45] Besides the fact that marijuana is illegal in most states, its usage contributes to the overall apathy of some students. The use of marijuana reduces the effort that people put into their schoolwork, causing professors to lower the academic standards if enough students are unable to keep up with the standards of the past generations. Therefore, these substances should be considered as unacceptable as alcohol. Furthermore, the use of "vaping" technologies has grown in popularity, sending students and young people alike into hospitals.[46] These e-cigarettes are now widely used among college students, and the only positive to them is that they are turning students away from smoking actual cigarettes. But they still have their downsides. From the dorm rooms and bathroom stalls to the classrooms and libraries, vaping is becoming more and more prevalent with surveys stating that students claimed that almost 80 percent of their peers had vaped within the past month.[47] During high school students would take bathroom breaks just to vape. I would walk into a cloudy bathroom smelling like Fruit Loops just trying to relieve myself, and this same phenomenon occurred when I entered university. However, students were discrete in higher education. I would see students vaping while walking to class, and I would sometimes see strange puffs of smoke within lecture halls. A more nuanced debate has circulated around the use of vaping devices for the use of nicotine. Though the health problems with these are not yet fully understood, they should nonetheless be prohibited because they are not conducive to the academic goals of a university. Parties and events where such illegal activities are conducted should also be canceled if there is any suspicion that it would lead to the use of these substances. The universities need greater oversight when it comes to these affairs on and around their campus through greater use of campus police.

Within the strict liability policy to enforce the prohibition of alcohol and other substances on college campuses, there should be an appeal process, as constantly expelling people suspected of using or possessing the banned substances risks becoming authoritarian with university, with innocents becoming victims. The campus police force would most likely need to be increased to better implement such a policy. Most students who engage in this conduct have alcohol in their dorms, so universities need to make sure that students are aware of dorm checks by the police for prohibited substances like fraudulent identifications, alcohol, and illegal drugs. In addition, universities need to be in constant contact with the bars in the surrounding communities to enforce penalties for underaged drinking.

Alcohol and marijuana should not permeate the atmosphere of college. Instead it should be the abundance of educational resources and the pursuit of knowledge for future betterment of society that sets the mood. It is a perversion of the university to allow such widespread drinking on campuses, and it lowers the reputation that universities have in the communities. Students in their formative years, a time when they are still forming their decision-making mental faculties, should avoid alcohol and illegal substances. Universities who care about the actual mental development of their students need to enforce strict guidelines for this problem and ban the use of alcohol on campus and for those underage people off campus. If universities accomplish this very basic task, it will be a stepping stone to restore the prestige of American higher education.

Like with some of the other failures in higher education, there is a slight exception for top universities where the drinking and partying culture is not as pervasive for the student body. At these top of the top schools, drinking and partying are still major parts of the college experience, but they are less so than most other colleges where the culture is right in the face of most students. It is not that these universities are special in their enforcement of the rules regarding alcohol. Rather the student body is generally more concerned with other important aspects of college like studying and extra curriculars. It does not mean that these students are fully mature either, for they too engage in heavy drinking and partying, however, it is to a lower degree than other universities.

The university needs to gain control over the substances like alcohol, marijuana, and tobacco on the campus itself and in the surrounding areas not only because it leads to a degradation of the higher education system but also because it leads to student engagement in more illegal conduct. There are second and third order effects of the use of these substances. More people will assault others physically and sexually. Injuries from these idiotic activities abound when students engage in drinking alcohol and marijuana, putting themselves and others in danger. A major consequence of not controlling just these basic substances within the higher education system is that universities are essentially allowing students to progress into harder forms of drugs and substances. Because under-age drinking and marijuana use abounds, it allows for some students who are already under the influence to maintain a propensity to take other, harsher substances. In this manner, alcohol and marijuana are gateway substances. Though I am not claiming that all uses of alcohol and marijuana lead to other substances, I am merely noting that the absence of the former will make it more difficult for the latter to be used. If the students are not already under the influence, they should have more common sense when being confronted with things like cocaine or mushrooms. Prohibited substances, like alcohol, should be more taboo in greater society because of its many detrimental effects. One of the oddest things you see in university is that some alcohol companies sponsor university events like football games. Universities are absolutely failing in the composition of a substance-free system to the absolute detriment of the student body. It is one of the more serious failures of higher education, leading to the death of students, and it is time universities began to pay more attention to this scourge.

Chapter VIII

Promiscuity and Hookup Culture

"Men are more moral than they think and far more immoral than they can imagine."—Sigmund Freud

In the past forty years, the number of college students who were married went from more than half in the 1980s to single digits in the modern era. In effect, this is the result of modern generations delaying marriage at an increasing rate.[48] Correspondingly, this generation is more sexually active than previous ones. The former generations emphasis on double standards regarding promiscuity of men and women is a thing of the past, demonstrated by roughly the same levels of sexual activity of genders of today compared with the imbalance of the past. Previously, men and women generally getting married right after college or already married before entering, but wanting to have as much fun through promiscuity before settling down is now the atmosphere of the youth.[49] This is going to get worse as the student loan crisis is magnified over time because people tend to put off marriage as a result of massive crippling debt burdens.

As more youths push off marriage, there is a corresponding increase in promiscuous behavior, especially within higher education. A recent study demonstrated that 91% of university students claimed their life was dominated by the perceived hookup culture. This is a relative overestimation on the amount of sexual encounters students participate in during their college years as more statistics bear out that only seven out of ten students have engaged in a hookup.[50] But these facts establish that one's peer group is a major factor in determining socialization, and there is, in fact, a culture that promotes such behavior even though most college relationships are monogamous. The idea of seven out of ten college students hooking up during college does not necessarily alter the idea that hooking up does not pressure almost all college students. Many people in college would engage in such activities if they had the opportunity. But, for a certain amount of people, usually men, this is not an option because of their perceived value in the unregulated sexual marketplace. The sexual value of these men is not high enough so most women will not give them the opportunity for engaging in hookup culture. Even though these men feel intense pressure to engage in such conduct, they cannot, so it skews the statistics, making it seem as though there is a select group of voluntary chaste individuals. Still there are those individuals who voluntarily avoid engaging in this conduct. I was one of those people for most of my time in college, but there is still a repressive culture of immoral sexual freedom that is leading to a degradation of the collective university student society.

There are volumes of data backing the relationship between alcohol and this hookup culture. In fact, 64% of students recorded that alcohol was in the equation of the hookup. Moreover, 80% of college students utilized alcohol in support of making the encounter that led to the hookup.[51] The odd thing about these interactions is that the communication between the parties is generally an issue and the expression of emotions for both parties are clouded. These "friends with benefits" relationships make it difficult to set ground rules that do not tie emotions into the mix, and many who engage in such activities view emotions for the other as a negative consequence. Moreover, a vast majority—almost three quarters—expresses dissatisfaction with the hookup interactions, and while most feel physically satisfied, they do not feel emotionally satisfied. In these types of dynamic relationships, there is a propensity for unwanted sexual experiences. A study found that 77% of unwanted sexual contact described by the survey participants occurred within the context of a hookup relationship.[52] Generally, too, there is a discontent between perceived outcomes in that around half of men and women thought that the hookup would turn into a relationship, causing emotional distress when things did not play out that way.

As the use of technology grows, dating apps are taking center stage in the hookup culture arena as more and more college students use devices to perpetuate their promiscuous behavior. There are those who use these apps for monogamous relationships, but the overall culture regarding these apps feeds into the "friends with benefits" outcomes that leaves most who participate emotionally deprived. Proponents of dating apps still claim that they are just avenues for those who were already promiscuous to continue with that lifestyle, but many people who go onto these apps are socially timid when approaching the other gender for hookup, so it gives them greater opportunity to actually proceed with such activities.

Some researchers claim that there is no problem with the casual hookup culture itself. Instead it is the compulsion students feel if they do not engage in such behavior. On one end of the spectrum, college students can feel socially isolated in the prevailing culture of hooking up, and on the other end, they can be thrown into the harsh emotional landscape of casual relationships.[53] There is merit to this idea with both ends of the spectrum causing problems for students, but which one is worse? Feeling socially isolated from an activity that everyone is engaging in is difficult but engaging in promiscuous behavior because you do not want to be isolated is not necessarily beneficial. These types of relationships cause second and third order effects that ripple throughout the college community, perpetuating the culture, and causing harm to participants.

The solution to the high number of sexual assaults on campus, of which about twenty percent of women and five percent of men are victims,[54] could lie in the dismantling of this type of culture where emotions and common chivalry are disjoined from one other. If the culture of not aligning emotional and physical pleasures continues to persist, there will be sexual misconduct that results in either assault or extreme disappointment. The act of hooking up is not just a physical act of pleasure, but it has scientific chemical responses in the brain to which people become attached. Usually college students report that past hookups were regrettable. So, becoming emotionally tied with a person that you regrettably hookup with is not the wisest decision. There is a movement to treat sexual conduct as just another bodily function, but it is so much more profound than that simplistic definition. There are major consequences to sexual conduct, and students should be far more careful with their actions than they are currently.

It is difficult to introduce a top-down approach to this problem because there is no real way that universities or governments can quell the free, voluntary decisions of those above the age of 18 when it comes to sexual conduct. The focus on universities has been to try to solve the consequences of the problem, the symptoms of the disease, like they do with the problem of alcohol. They focus on making sure students have protected sex with the use of contraceptive, and they make a concerted effort to define consent in the atmosphere where most college students have a propensity to binge drink. These are commendable policies and noble pursuits, but universities need to address the overall culture that is at the heart of the problem. Universities should also discuss with their students the statistics to end the perpetuation of the culture. They need to enlighten students on the idea that not everyone is engaging in this behavior. The parents of college students need to educate their children on the ramifications of hooking up and the possible results of such conduct. Yet, individuals themselves must hold themselves to a higher standard and recognize that the mere act of hooking up has other ramifications past the purely physical.

Universities should consider teaching the ideals of a successful marriage as well as protecting people from Sexually Transmitted Diseases (STD) and defining consent under the influence of alcohol. They should teach about what goes into a good marriage and what supports the family unit, which is where most formative education of children takes place before high school and college. College students need to understand the differences between interests and values. Many young people are approaching relationships with the idea that similar interests are the foundation that makes long term relationships work. In fact, it is the similar values that make relationships last. With the divorce rate high in the modern era, it is important for college students to understand that relationships must have strong mutual agreement on major ideas and interpretations of the world in religious, moral, and ideological stances. Having a solid marriage is a necessity to this ideal, and the hookup culture that dominates the campus is not conducive to students who plan to contribute to humanity and raise productive citizens to the country and the world.

From personal experience, this culture is as pervasive on college campuses as the consumption of alcohol; not everyone engages in the activity, but many do. Those who do lead the culture set the standard. One of the things that I believe perpetuates the hookup culture and enhanced promiscuity on campus are the organizations of fraternities and sororities. In the past, the hookup culture on campus was confined to these organizations, but they are now at the forefront for propagating it throughout the main student body. I am referring to fraternal organizations that have no other goal than a collection of the same gender for the purpose of friendship and connections. There are positive fraternities that engage in the pursuit of knowledge and charity, but most of the Greek organizations do not have such purposes in mind. Those that throw formals and, maybe once a year, do some service to the community contribute to the overall atmosphere of hooking up rather than following academic pursuits. I never understood these organizations and would be puzzled at the sight of women, who have never met each other, acting like they were family. This might be nice for participants and help them gain more friends, but why would someone need to pay hundreds of dollars, even thousands, depending on the university, to participate in such activities. Fraternities and sororities contribute to the hookup culture in this manner on campuses. Their parties, gatherings, and overall demeanor propagate a hookup and drinking culture on college campuses because of their leading roles in those activities. The university system should take a hard and serious look at disbanding these organizations that do not contribute to the overall educational goals of the university. It is not the point of college to have an organization with the overall goal of friendship and partying.

Tangentially related to the hookup culture on college campuses is the subsequent rise in pornography consumption of the youth. The availability of such content has led to many more young people consuming it. A research team has looked into this increase to discover that from the 1970s to the 2000s, the consumption of pornography increased 16 percent in men.[55] There are a great many issues with pornography, like decreasing sexual satisfaction, loneliness, and divorce, which are some of the issues that lead to poor relationships. In effect, this adds to the promiscuity and hookup culture on college campuses because the monogamy of relationships is deteriorating, thus, making the "friends with benefits" relationship look more appealing.[56] Introducing pornography to the youth is becoming more of an issue as access to internet is widespread, and parents need to be very aware of the dangers of pornography usage on the youth. The solution to pornography use and its detrimental effects for those above the age of eighteen goes back to personal responsibility. The government cannot usurp the freedom of viewing such material, as that would be worse than the effects via violation of many constitutional rights. Censorship is not the right course of action. Instead, students taking responsibility to not degrade themselves with excessive pornography usage is one of the ways the hookup culture might be solved. Parents need to take more of an active role in making sure that their children are not using internet capable devices for such activities.

The advent of birth control in the 1960s is a relatively new thing in the world, and the effects of this game changing invention are only marginally known. For the first time in history, women can control their reproduction processes, and there are new sets of rules that go along with this development. What are those rules? At the invention's beginning in the 60s, the rule was to party, celebrate, and engage in promiscuity, as the bad consequences of such actions seemed to disappear. Fast forward to today and it is clear the family unit has been harmed to a considerable extent, and there still is barely any discussion on the parameters regarding sexual interactions. The rules of the past were simple: Do not have sexual intercourse until marriage. But reliable birth control has destroyed that rule for most people in the modern era, at least in the Western Hemisphere and especially on college campuses. More college students are beginning to say that sexual interactions with others are not consensual if you regret that interaction the next day or some period after the interaction. There is a major contradiction with the youth on campuses too. College students want to engage in whatever sexual interactions they want with whomever they want, whenever they want, and without any problems in the area of consent. But it is very difficult to actually define consent if the guiding ethos is simply that college students can do whatever sexual conduct they want under whatever circumstances. You cannot have both of those things. There needs to be an in-depth analysis on what circumstances are appropriate to give consent. Many on the radical left of the political spectrum argue that there must be consent at every level. Each party must give verbal consent, sign a contract outlining parameters, and stamp it with a royal seal each time they touch someone else. This is so mind-numbingly awkward. Consent is obviously a necessity in any sexual encounter, but people must be able to have some sense of social cues. While college is a time to explore sexuality and sexual interaction, students need to be far more careful of their sexual behavior. Students need to realize that if they participate in this culture, they deviate from a strong social pressure for long-term monogamy at their own detriment.[57] Society needs to reevaluate the standards of sexual practice, especially on college campuses, where there is an overwhelming hookup culture. The hookup culture on college campuses debases the value of everyone's physical and emotional state, and it is going to take a long time and major societal discourse to produce a solution to this problem.

It is difficult to predict the future of such a hookup culture because any grouping of young adults with questionable decision-making skills and an abundance of alcohol will result in obvious sexual encounters. However, as university moves online and usual encounters between the sexes are formed through dating apps, students will hopefully focus more on meaningful relationships that align the physical with the emotional. But I do not see a change in the future unless there is greater personal responsibility adopted by each young adult in the community to cherish traditional relationships over instant gratification.

Chapter IX

The Plague of Social Media

"Vanity pushes a man to ridiculous boasting and hypocrisy."
—Aesop

I f anyone were to sit in on a college class before the instruction began, they would look around to see barely any communication between students. There would maybe be some people talking to each other, maybe discussing the course at hand. But, usually, most students are glued to their phones, paying close attention to their social media accounts like Facebook, Snapchat, Twitter, or Instagram. I am by no means exempted from this, as I would from time to time browse my phone before class began, however, I began to stop myself and wonder what the point of social media and why was I spending so much time on it. Why do some people put more effort into these accounts than real relationships, and why are so many college students engaged in these social media accounts?

In a recent Pew Research Center survey, social media use was most common in the generation of 18-29 year olds where about 88% of them were using some form of social media. The differences in platform use was notable in that 78% of 18-24 year olds were Snapchat users, while this tapers off to 54% with 25-29 year olds. Facebook is still the dominant social media for most Americans, but platforms like Instagram, Twitter, and Snapchat are the largest for the younger generations. A majority of social media users would say that it would not be difficult to give up these sites, but a majority of the users of these sites visit them on a daily basis.[58] In regards to college students, approximately 27 percent of students use social media more than six hours a week in 2014, which is an increase from 20 percent in 2007. Students are now spending less face to face time with their peers, which gives rise to the idea that social media is harmful to relationships. [59]

One of the largest problems for college students within higher education is their mental health, and anxiety is the most predominant at about 41 percent being plagued with the illness, followed by 36 percent being depression and 35 percent being relationship issues.[60] Mental health on college campuses is a growing concern, but what is the cause of these students' anxiety in such an environment where universities try to coddle students and the academic standards for the past thirty years have significantly dropped? It is argued that the beginning of the issue of increased rates of depression and anxiety began around 2012 or 2013, which perfectly coincides with the popularization of smartphones and increased social media usage.[61] Now, the university system obviously puts pressure on students with the workload and the pressure to be perfect for the professors and friends, but I think that social media is increasing the rates of depression and anxiety, which magnify mental illness for college students because they use it so much. Suicide is the second leading cause of college student death after alcohol.[62] Pressure from school work, jobs, families, relationships, and professors all coincide to make for a stressful life, but most of those things come along with the college experience of pursuing knowledge beyond yourself. Social media is an expendable aspect of college students' lives that is an anxiety inducing plague. It's easy for a student looking at social media to feel weak or low on the dominance hierarchy because the levels of competency are so mind-numbingly high that it is very unlikely that you are the greatest at a single domain of competency. The brain assigns a lower place on the hierarchy, limiting the amount of serotonin in the brain, causing more negative feelings as a result of social media usage. Numerous studies have displayed the effects of social media, and they have discovered a causal link between social media and feelings of depression.[63] The fear of missing out is also a big aspect of the negative effects of social media where people only post very interesting things, and the viewers wish they could be doing the same.

I had multiple social media accounts during my college experience, and I realized how much time I was wasting watching things that had nothing to do with my path in life. Furthermore, the sites were taking away time that I could have used for building closer relationships outside of social media. I deleted my Snapchat, which I realized was pointless because text messaging someone was essentially the same, so the app was superfluous to my life. Also, I barely use my only other social media account, which is an Instagram. All social media accounts want you to stay on their sites as long as possible to make money through ads and other services, so they cater to you through algorithms that entice you to continue using them. As they began to take out significant portions of my day, I decided to stop using them. These sites do have further repercussions on mental health because I felt pressured to post things when seeing others continuing to live such great lives. It is a feeling of many of my young friends and a major problem within the higher education system. There is a reason why most successful people come from small towns for it was far easier to be the best in such a location. With social media spreading, it becomes far harder to view yourself as a success.

However, there is a special place for YouTube in my heart when it comes to my disdain for social media and its negative effects on society, particularly college students. The site is a great platform for sharing videos, which have genres that include educational content, like documentaries and lectures. Although it still has videos that could lead to viewers feeling lonely or depressed, it uses algorithms to find what the person wants to watch. It is moving away from a social media platform to overtake television and compete with streaming platforms like Netflix or Hulu. It is one of the best sites for free information because the video aspect makes it easier than reading, so it can share massive amounts of information to those wanting to learn on a budget. YouTube is less of a social media platform because it does not have that emphasis of having friends or profiles, but the focus is instead on the content being shared. Therefore, this is less of a sense of fear of missing out or the idea that you are lower on the dominance hierarchy because you can look for videos that you want to see, like educational content.

Outside of useful social media like YouTube, and possibly LinkedIn, I view most other forms of social media as horrible time wasters. They do not really add to the life of the user except for feelings of depression. There are benefits of social media like staying in contact with older friends, but the negatives outweigh this benefit. Moreover, staying in contact with people is not the point of many platforms of social media. The aim of these sites is to post pictures and feelings rather than the direct messaging between users. It was assumed that social media would be able to connect the world, which is done via the internet, but friendships where real connections are created have decreased as a result of social media. The internet is a great place for communication and information, but the social sector of life must not be overtaken entirely with these sites that do not add the individual's life or relationships. Social media is even leading to political division, where parties are becoming more polarized as a result of social media algorithms creating ideological echo chambers.[64] Social media is becoming even more of a monster when they are taking mass data collection from the users to then sell that information to third parties.[65] These companies are growing so large with so many users that they can effectively silence people through deactivation of accounts. They are on the two sides of the same coin: They can spread words of revolution that lead to the collapse of dictatorship but can also suppress the freedom of expression, leading to a particular person of an ideology to win an election in a democracy. Small yet impactful effects have been seen with social media swaying elections and propagating revolutions, especially during the Arab Spring.

The social media platforms are given power based in large part on the people who use them, and a significant amount of the youth in America use these sites as an integral part of their lives. Young people, especially those in university where people are already suffering from high levels of anxiety, should desert, not the vast wealth of knowledge of the internet, but social media. Universities should encourage lower social media use, and they need to point out the dangers of social media on the mental state of the individual. The internet and many sites that involve a social component are very useful to college students, but social media like Twitter, Snapchat, and Facebook need to be thrown out by university students because they take away from better in-person relationships. They waste time that could be used for working or studying during university. The social media boom arguably began on college campuses with Facebook as a way to interact with other students within higher education, but it has morphed into a grotesque embodiment of envy and arbitrary authoritarian policy that leads to less in-person relationships and higher rates of depression and anxiety in young people. A very radical step for universities is to block such sites within their Wi-Fi, but students would get around this easily, and it diminishes the freedom of individuals. Thus, college students and young people need to take it upon themselves to not involve themselves in this competition to post the best picture or the most inspiring tweets. Studying and working hard will make your life better in the long run, not endlessly scrolling through social media for hours, looking at staged photographs of people supposedly living a better life than you.

Chapter X

Postmodern Indoctrination and Safe Space Ideology

"Give me four years to teach the children and the seed I have sown will never be uprooted."—Vladimir Lenin

I f you are paying tuition for a liberal arts degree, or you are paying your taxes, you are supporting radical ideologues that despise Western civilization as an oppressive patriarchal structure. These destructive individuals are the professors at many universities that resent Western society and its values, promulgating nihilist theories through their lectures and courses. They are what many call the postmodernists, who actively seek to influence directly and indirectly the political identity of students on campus. This postmodern indoctrination is churning out masses of liberal-thinking graduates who go forth trying to overthrow the West and capitalism. This movement is the cause of far-left agendas witnessed on college campuses around the country. The scene of radical mobs trying to shut down invited controversial guests is an increasingly common occurrence. Codes of speech are now becoming a trend in which offensive speech is labeled as "hate speech." Politically correct verbiage is stifling free-flowing ideas and debates that universities were designed to propagate. Universities spend tuition and tax dollars to fund diversity training and administer this type of diversity through a totalitarian top-down approach. What makes this even worse is that students are incurring debt for this type of teaching. They are not learning how to learn skeptically or to think for themselves. They are being indoctrinated in order to have a singular viewpoint and proliferate the far leftist agenda of these professors.

During the 1960s, these true believers of the postmodern ideology became professors, and they are teaching the ideas of their postmodern thesis, which have diversity and equality as their cornerstones. But there are major issues with this worldview of theirs that is being pummeled into students, particularly in the liberal arts and humanities. Diversity is not what you would expect it to mean. It is not diversity of opinion and background. Rather, it is based on ethnicity, race, and gender. These postmodern professors and the students who follow their ideology do not differentiate between equality of outcome and equality of opportunity. They believe that all inequity is inequality. They desire the equality of outcome more than equality of opportunity, an outlook that is destructive to a democratic and free society. The problem with these two fundamentals of postmodernism is that they see other opinions as violence rather than simply incorrect. They view opposing opinions as a propagation of Western oppression and racism. They do not believe that reasonable people will come to reasonable conclusions based on fact, so they must quell any opposing voice. Moreover, the postmodernists adopt a neo-Marxist view of the world in which the capitalist structure of the west, which has brought hundreds of millions of people out of poverty, is a moral evil to be destroyed. They disdain the voluntary transactions of the people of a free society and curse the meritocracy that a free economy breeds.

One of the most distressing aspects of the postmodern ideology is the focus on identity politics and intersectionality. They classify people, not as individuals with distinct ideas, passions, and political viewpoints, but as the manifestation of their race, sexual orientation, or gender. They view the world as a civilization of oppressors and victims, which produces nothing more than division between separate groups, particularly of race and ethnicity. These ideas were manifested in countries around the world in the latter half of the 20th century through socialism and communism, and the results were the complete failure of economies and tens of millions of deaths. The United States fought decades against the ideas that are now rising on college campuses in the new form of identity politics. This is an ever-growing feedback loop as society keeps sending their children to these institutions to be brainwashed. And, if continued, the ideology will spread from the university to America and the entire western world.[66]

In 2007, the most exhaustive study of the political leanings of professors in America's higher education system was completed with some interesting results. The study found that 44 percent of professors were liberal, and 46 percent were moderate while only about 9 percent were conservative.[67] Community colleges displayed some slight differences from the four-year university in that about 19 percent were conservative and 37 percent were liberal. The largest proportion of liberal professors was found in liberal arts colleges that had 61 percent of their professors espousing liberal ideology. Nationally, a 2014 study demonstrated that the liberal to conservative professor ratio was six to one, and that same research noted that the ratio was more pronounced in New England where it was 28 to 1. There was a more recent study in 2016 that analyzed responses from 40 major American universities. It found that the ratio of Democrat to Republican professors was about 4.5 to 1 in the field of economics. But, shockingly, there is a ratio of 33.5 to 1 in the field of history. A liberal bias among professors does not necessarily translate to professors brainwashing their students.

However, a 2016 Pew Research Center study found that of those who attend some form of graduate school, there were 31 percent who *consistently* hold liberal positions and 23 percent who hold *mostly* liberal positions, compared to only about 10 percent holding *consistently* conservative principles and 17 holding *mostly* conservative principles. There is a clear correlation between gaining more university education and holding more liberal ideology. This is because the overwhelming postmodernist ideology reigns on college campuses, and those who ascribe to these ideas will be more inclined to gain more of the education that they have agreed with during their time in higher education. It is essentially a postmodern feedback loop in undergrad and graduate schools as conservatives are more likely to pursue other professional fields like an MBA instead of a liberal-inclined Ph.D. Conservatives are not shut out from university education through some discriminatory practice, but they are far less likely to end up in academia. This is a result of liberals being much more likely to consider a PhD due to their absorption with the postmodern, neo-Marxist, and identity politics taught by professors in the liberal arts and humanities during their undergraduate education.[68]

Safe spaces are one of the consequences of the postmodern ideology. Viewpoints of others arbitrarily deemed offensive, particularly those views on the right wing, are silenced. Safe spaces are where students must not say anything that offends others, creating a lack of diverse viewpoints on controversial topics.[69] This is antithetical to the goal of university because in order to think one, must risk offending others. If the topic of discussion is important, the probability that you will not offend anybody is nil. The safe space ideology makes students into what is now commonly called "snowflakes." They are not being prepared for the real world, which does not necessarily care too much about postmodern ideas. The real world cares far more about economic productivity. Out of the safe space ideology comes the idea of political correctness. It is essentially where there became an infinite number of ways to define a finite number of objective aspects. It places the objective truth at a lower position than the feelings of others. By nature, people within the western world are usually polite to each other, and most people do not seek to harm their fellow citizens. However, political correctness fogs the issues at hand from rational apprehension, so complex issues cannot be solved. It halts reasonable debate and conversation about topics in the political discourse, essentially stifling freedom of speech. Being victims of speech that is controversial will lead to people not taking control of their personal responsibility. The road to getting back to the freedom of speech that universities should foster is to speak freely and clearly articulate truth without overthinking the consequences.

From personal experience, I noticed the liberal biases

85

more so in my history classes than other required courses. Postmodern identity politics, except the classes taught by professors who were over the age of eighty, heavily influenced my political science courses. A great deal of students would not even discuss issues relating to a controversial topic, and they would end the conversation as soon as they felt uncomfortable. People on campuses are pushing back because this safe space idea has taken on an Orwellian form. Not discussing controversial topics or allowing all viewpoints is a very dreadful journey that people do not want to travel down.

The only consensus of conservative thought I discovered, outside of clubs and organizations designed for conservatives, was ROTC, where many were on the right wing of the political spectrum. But, the idea of universities is not just to have monoliths of single political thought. It is to have a diversity of opinion to which people can discuss ideas without worrying that feelings can be harmed. A safe space ideology was essentially absent in ROTC, providing for a breath of fresh air of conversation and productive intellectual sparring. Outside of this program, the postmodern and safe space ideology was infused in the campus culture. For example, my university administration was criticized for having a lack of diversity in the candidates for the search of a new university president. They protested the candidate list not because of qualifications or lack of diversity of opinion but because of the color of the candidates' skin. This was the prime example of identity politics on my college campus that made me question the postmodern gospel my professors had taught.

Along with this ideology, many students try to fight

against the so-called "patriarchy" where men are thought to reign supreme, especially men who are white and western. They are Don Quixote fighting the windmills of a sexist society in America. Almost everything in the social order can be classified as sexist to these students, and those who are not women seemingly cannot present statistics or have an opinion. From personal experience, I have been called sexist before for noting the differences between men and women, which for the postmodernists do not exist. However, this doctrine is simply erroneous. Men and women differ by temperament at the extremes of the bell curves. Nine out of ten people who are in prisons are men, and there are biological reasons for that disparity. The two genders are generally the same, but the differences come out on the extremes where the most disagreeable people are almost all men and the most agreeable people are almost all women. Noting these basic facts is not sexist. However, many students virtue signal and pat themselves on the back by calling others sexist who dare note the facts. If universities are unable to report statistics and make inferences based on them at the risk of contradicting the postmodern ideology, then there is no point of a university. The university cannot increase the aggregate of human wisdom under this type of totalitarian system.

Another aspect of fighting against the patriarchy for these postmodern leftists is the idea of toxic masculinity. This idea is pervasive in the modern university, but what does it exactly mean? Why is there no toxic femininity? Here is a major problem with these terms: They do not have a strict definition. And strict definitions inextricably matter. Many people claim that the idea of toxic masculinity is the outward movement against appropriate behavior for the masculine gender. It is a deviation of the actions that society deems right for men. But, if this were true, then there would be aspects of gender that were universally true, which is something that the postmodernists usually argue against. They usually claim that gender is malleable, something that can shift based on personal, subjective experience. However, you cannot have it both ways. Therefore, there is no such thing as toxic masculinity that does not include a subsequent toxic femininity. This is common sense as both genders can be toxic. The simple answer to solve both is generally the adherence to the social contract between righteous human beings, or benevolence regardless of the gender.

It is becoming increasingly popular to play the identity politics game where people, mainly on the left end of the political spectrum, attribute the group identity to the individual. They then ascribe victimhood and blame to different groups based on a perception of history. This is one of the most reprehensible ideologies people have ever designed. It is one of tenets of the postmodern ways of thinking where the group is primary, and the individual is secondary. This line of logic leads down a slippery slope very quickly, and there are no shortages of examples of placing the group over the individual in the 20th century from Nazi Germany to the USSR to communist China. It is one of the aspects of the postmodern ideology that needs to be combated by more students on college campuses because it is so detrimental to the overall fabric of the society itself.

Moral posturing or virtue signaling is another pervasive issue within higher education. The postmodern approach holds that those who express their high morals outwardly are cleansed of any wrongdoing. It is the church of social affirmation of moral value. There is a great book called *Ordinary Men* by Christopher Browning in which he discusses the police battalions moving into the conquered territories after the invading armies of the Third Reich. He lays bare how evil regular people can become in certain situations. The moral posturing of postmodernists on campuses outwardly displays a lack of personal understanding of themselves, for if they really knew how evil they could be, they would not be virtue signaling. It is a very upsetting thing to analyze oneself. To understand how cruel humanity can be and that you, at any time could be a part of that is a troubling thought. College students who ascribe to virtue signaling need to understand this dichotomy in the human spirit to be both evil and benevolent, and outward expression of how morally superior one is will not rid the soul of this dichotomy. The youth of today try to outwardly display their virtue through social media, but they are really displaying how little they know about human nature and themselves.

Cancel culture is another movement that is a partial consequence of the postmodern ideology. This is where mobs of virtue signaling crusaders try to demolish those that do not agree with the mainstream idea or say something outside the leftist student's dogma. They will harass people in person, but the harassment turns especially bold when they go online because of the increased anonymity. People need to try to communicate with others online as they would in person. There needs to be a path to redemption for those who committed wrongs in the past instead of simply mobbing them, trying to destroy their lives for a supposed wrong they committed in the past. What the postmodernists are doing is ascribing the ethical standards of today to those in the past, prosecuting them today for the wrongs of the past. Things that were not viewed as racist in the past are now resurfacing as offensive to people, usually white liberals. And these mobs then try to destroy the individual because of these past violations. Even more, they begin toppling statues of people who were generally good for American history like Thomas Jefferson or George Washington. For the postmodernist, it will never be enough. The mobs rule, and it will be a continual sense of outrage as the individual is never woke enough.

All the things I have claimed here are commonly held views, however, many people are usually silent on these topics out of fear of repercussions of the leftist mob that dominates college campuses at the propagation of postmodern professors. It is horrible that students come into university not having any idea about what to politically think. So, they choose majors in the humanities, and they are filled with this ideology. Then, they are kicked in the teeth when they graduate with massive debt and an ideology that does not serve them at all. They become resentful of the system of meritocracy, reaffirming their hatred of capitalism. They must find a job and pay taxes on top of that. They once thought taxes were just something for the rich to pay their fair share, but not anymore.

Chapter XI

Affirmative Action and The Affluent

"We are not rich by what we possess but by what we can do without." —Immanuel Kant

The differentiation in allocating resources to sets of people based on their group identity because of past discrimination is the policy of affirmative action. One of the growing trends in university admissions is to include lower standards for specific minorities because of past injustices to a group. Standardized tests, which are used as an objective resource for intelligence, are now trying to include a race or ethnicity component that alters the score arbitrarily based on the group identity of the individual. The proponents of this admissions process claim that the admission of students should not be based solely on the academics of students but on a holistic approach taking everything into consideration from background to extracurriculars. Because of its focus on race and a singular postmodern bias against supposedly oppressive white men and other ethnicities and races, it has led some people to question the standards. Why would it be fair for an Asian student who is qualified while poor to be rejected in favor of an under-qualified African American who comes from a wealthy family?[70] This dilemma at the heart of affirmative action is that it attributes a group identity to the particular individual, and it ascribes blame to an entire group of another race. This is a postmodern ideology, and it is a failure of higher education to live up to the standards of pure scholarship.

Generally, people do not want to address the subject because it is controversial. People immediately call those who do not agree with the policy a racist; these people do not engage with others who have different views. However, we need to get at the heart of this problem for it is actually discriminatory itself. There was a recent lawsuit filed against Harvard University by a group of Asian-American students who were rejected from the school because of race considerations. The court ruled in favor of Harvard, arguing that they use many other parameters when evaluating an applicant, like geographic background and income, and race, therefore, is not much different. They did not violate any civil rights by using these metrics in their system of admissions. The plaintiffs filed an appeal, one likely not going to go anywhere.[71] Of course, university admissions should not be solely based on test scores and GPA, and there are benefits of having a diverse student body, but it should focus on personal achievement and not race, ethnicity, geography, gender, or sexual orientation. Many critics of affirmative action call it reverse discrimination, but that term is fallacious as it is just simply discrimination. It does not matter who is discriminating against whom; it is still discrimination. Currently, affirmative action was upheld in the Supreme Court decision in *Grutter v. Bollinger,* while the idea of racial quotas in college admissions was ruled unconstitutional by

Affirmative Action and The Affluent

Gratz v. Bollinger. [72] [73]

We cannot fix the racist past or erase the history of racism. This is not to dismiss individual acts of racism that are abhorrent to any sensible mind. But the use of minorities for tokens of diversity leads to huge problems down the line. Even though affirmative action is done in good faith, one problem is that it creates a system where some students who would have been successful at other schools are then moved by affirmative action into more academically challenging environments where they are more likely to fail out. The dropout rate for African Americans is twice that of their white peers, and there is also a correlation of higher dropouts to those admitted with a legacy influence. It is not that these minorities are getting bullied out of the university through racism; those that dropout just generally cannot handle the challenging academic environment. In the mid-1990s, the state of California instituted a policy where race, sex, color, ethnicity, or national origin would not constitute a basis for preferential treatment. When this order went into place, this type of academic mismatching lowered as different public universities in the state only offered admissions based on the actual records of the students.[74] The dropout rate decreases when you appropriately place students in the best university for them rather than arbitrarily placing them in certain universities based on race. Affirmative action is the antithesis of what Martin Luther King Jr. argued for in the 1960s that people not be judged by the color of their skin but for the value they provide to the community.

There should not be any other factors that come into play in the admissions process other than the individual's academic and personal record. Accordingly, the idea of legacy, whether your parents or grandparents went to that university, should also not be a consideration. It does not matter that an applicant's parents went to that university; it has nothing to do with the personal and academic accomplishments of the student. Further, the idea that being a "first generation college student" should not be a part of the admissions process. Usually, these applicants get a boost in their admissions rate, and they are sometimes given generous scholarships. The reason for this is because it assumes that if one's parents did not attend higher education, the parents must be poor or uneducated. Therefore, the applicant must have had a difficult life. It assumes that college is the best pathway for all people, and it is the golden ticket to a better life. It assumes that the only way for people to become educated is through university. These assumptions are simply not the case anymore, and this aspect of the admissions process should be left in the past where it belongs.

The family unit is one of the greatest predictors of educational success. Single parent homes are far less likely to produce more time for children to focus on studying as the parent is working and doing other things. Society at large should bring more attention to the education of children within the family before sending them to universities to become brainwashed. Parents teach their children valuable skills and culture that will either aid in the pursuit of education or hamper it, and it is not the government's job to step into admissions of higher education to rectify the past injustices of the society. Sometimes, affirmative action is based on the socioeconomic status of the individual, assuming they met the requisite requirements of the university. All other things being equal, a student who comes from a low-income area who achieves the same test scores and GPA as someone who came from a high-income area should be given better treatment. Although this is good in principle that should be a material component to the admissions process, it is difficult to productively institute such a policy. It is hard to quantify the burden that the student has overcome throughout his or her life. Basing this decision on race or the amount of money your parents have is almost impossible. Things are not that black and white.

Defrauding the university admissions process using power, status, and wealth is just as loathsome as affirmative action. Recently, the Department of Justice unleashed the prosecution of the largest college admissions scam in history, where 50 people were caught in a cabal to gain spots at the top universities. They used wealth to the tune of millions of dollars to pay for higher test scores and back doors into elite universities through sports scholarships for sports they didn't even play, going as far as doctoring photos to make it seem like they were accomplished athletes. Wealthy parents, in some instances, paid coaches and administrators to secure positions through outright bribery. Students who were rejected with qualifying academic and personal standards are rightly upset, and some are even suing the universities.[75] Though I doubt these suits will go anywhere, this entire scheme of the wealthy demonstrates a need to reform universities and colleges in regard to the admissions process, as well as reducing the large bureaucracy.

This problem is getting worse as colleges become need-aware, a process where they include the applicant's wealth or parents' wealth in the admissions process. Instead of being need-blind where this information is absent, the admissions officers are considering these factors in the decision. Conspicuous acceptance follows when prospective students' parents provide a large donation to universities. For example, Jared Kushner was admitted to Harvard following his father's donation of $2.5 million to the university.[76] The wealthy should not get preferential treatment when it comes to their admissions. It needs to be based solely off accomplishments, achievements, and academic prowess. Some argue though that it is a positive for universities to prefer students from rich families. They claim that it is a positive because it allows for the subsidization of less fortunate individuals without money. Also, it provides the extra income for sports like swimming that do not necessarily rake in the cash as much as football.[77] This is absurd; the wealth of a particular family should not come into the admissions process at all; even if they subsidies others, it allows for a slippery slope where the affluent can simply buy their way into top universities. Moreover, university, again back to its fundamental goals, is about the repository of human knowledge and the pursuit of it; if the prospective student does not have the academic and accomplishments to progress the goals of the university, they should not be accepted. Just like in the economy, if you do not have the skills required to perform a job or expand the company you should not be hired.

In general, I believe the current university admissions process is capricious nonsense. In its current form, it is just a selection tool used to make their degree worth something. If everyone were able to attend these universities, then there would be too many people who have the degree. It would not mean as much as it did when few people had it. Regardless, debating this issue with universities regarding their admissions will become insignificant in the coming decades. As accreditation moves elsewhere and as information online continues to abound, the university admissions process, as we know it, will no longer exist. Success will not look like being admitted to a top university. It will look like a person having the requisite qualifications for a career, not necessarily achieved through a university. It might look like scoring high on an accreditation test provided outside the halls of higher education. Graduate students might be the only few people left on campuses as many undergraduate academic fields, besides STEM students, move into an online setting. Universities rubber stamping the graduate as "educated" will go away as more people realize the information in college is online and graduating does not necessarily mean that you are educated. I do not think this will happen instantly, but the writing is on the wall. Regardless of whether universities will almost entirely be different in the coming years, the process in its current form usurps meritocracy, which is the basis of the free market. One's value determined by merit is increasingly absent in college admissions, and personal accomplishment and academic prowess need to take back the center stage.

Chapter XII

Individual Cost-benefit Analysis

"Price is what you pay. Value is what you get."—Warren Buffett

Throughout the 1600s, the plantation economy of Southern English America was gaining major ground, but, without the use of machinery in the colonies, they needed human labor to put in the work to profit on their agricultural endeavors. Despite slavery, the predominant system in the early new world was characterized by the headright system, which promised 50 acres of land to planters for every laborer brought over the Atlantic. So, planters would start bringing over laborers into the new world to profit off the system. This system seemed to benefit the laborers, labeled as indentured servants, who would be given a free ride across the Atlantic in exchange for their labor in a plantation for a specific number of years. They would then be released with a predetermined "freedom due" usually in land or other type of good. It was a harsh system and only about 40 percent of the servants survived the work term. The system would continue until Bacon's rebellion in 1676, when planters began preferring African slaves.[78] Though less physically harsh than the 17th century, this type of servitude is being perpetuated by the universities in the modern American higher education system through the use of student loans that are not absolvable in bankruptcy. Student loans must be paid off by those that took them out regardless of any other financial constraints. The administration of universities and colleges has conspired to steal the long-term salaries of the students through this process. As time goes on, the system just keeps getting worse as a negative financial feedback loop is created with more and more students enrolling in college.

About 70 percent of high school students go into college right after high school according to 2016 Department of Education statistics, which is an increase from 63 percent in 2000.[79] The total amount of student loans in the United States went from $345 billion in 2004 to $1.3 trillion in only thirteen years. Moreover, the average student loan debt of graduates in 2017 was $28,650, and the age group that held most of the debt burden is those between the ages of 35-49. Further, 20% of the borrowers were behind on their payments.[80] Thirty and forty-year olds hold the most amounts of debt even though when they went to university, tuition was much lower than it is today, interest being the main driver. When those people graduated, they did not owe as much as the current generation, but they kept postponing the loans, so they must pay more and more interest. In addition, the opportunity costs of delaying four years of employment in the workforce can cost thousands of dollars more depending on the career one exits college with. Further, universities charge fees for things one might not even use. Not to mention, the cost of course books, which is highly inflated.

The average difference in salary of an individual who

attends college and one who just completes high school is around $17,500.[81] Even after taxes, one would assume that it is a good deal because of the increase in salary, and that one would be able to reasonably pay off the debt within two or three years. This is far from the reality. The average borrower with the aforementioned amount of debt will take an average of 21 years to pay off their student loans.[82] Two decades is a long time to be trapped under loans that are not dischargeable in bankruptcy. Every month, the borrower must take out of his or her salary a specific amount to pay off the loans, which means it is essentially indentured servitude. You are trapped having to pay your hard work to the student loan. Due to people having to pay this burden, they are not able to place that money into a retirement fund or put the money into a mortgage. Furthermore, it is going to be much more difficult to pay off these loans unless you go to a top tier school like Harvard or Yale where the employment opportunities are marginally better than other schools. It is especially difficult for women, who have almost two-thirds of the debt burden, and they must postpone marriage and subsequent pregnancy at their detriment. For women, waiting to have children is sometimes challenging if they wait too long. Additionally, men and women from college tend to marry each other, which leads to a doubling of the debt and not necessarily a doubling the couple's income. This entwines them in this mess together in the early stages of their marriage, causing emotional distress and postponing multiple financial opportunities. Most graduates do not have the fiscal discipline to pay off these loans, so they end up in turmoil. It is not a math problem, but an emotional one. Most do not have the emotional fortitude to maintain a budget that allows them to pay off the debt in a timely manner. If you are struggling to pay off your debt, investigate Dave Ramsey's approach to becoming financial independent. He takes a snowball approach to crushing debt, and he has helped millions get out of their student loans through disciplined financial responsibility.

As a society, we wanted everyone to be college educated but no one to dig ditches. The government, partly because of the Cold War, started to give out loans to young people. They began to guarantee these loans in the case of insolvency. Would any reasonable person loan a 17 or 18-year-old thousands of dollars? You would get laughed out of the bank, but it is perfectly fine if you go to college because the government is securing the loan. So, it gives financial incentive for more and more loans. These loans are more secure than mortgages in that they do not fail. You can foreclose on a home, but you cannot declare bankruptcy on student loans. Wall Street has begun to reap benefits from student loans because they are so secure and provide profitable returns. Therefore, Wall Street encourages the government to send students to college, which leads to more loans in the system. It is a negative feedback loop with the government acting like a cartel, stealing the future earnings of the youth. It is so easy to encourage recent high school graduates to go to college because these young people do not know what they are doing, so they just sign the promissory notes and go to college because they think it is the right thing to do. Moreover, the parents further the process by cosigning the loans, and they are under the same presumption that their child will not be a success without a college diploma.

In the late 1980s, William Bennett, Secretary of Education for Reagan, wrote a piece for the New York Times concerning the growth of student loan debt. Now referred to as the Bennett hypothesis, his idea was that the more grants and loans the government gave to attend university, the greater the increase in the cost of tuition.[83] He was absolutely correct in his prediction. Because students come into university with loans from the government, there is no reason for universities to maintain fiscal discipline. The government will provide a loan for almost any amount to students going into higher education. This gives universities the ability to spend excessively because the government provides the upfront capital at whatever rate even though graduates will have to pay the bill. Further, the government will keep providing these loans because it thinks that everyone deserves one. This corrupt system has essentially created the student loan crisis as universities spend more and raise tuition, subsidized by the government and propagated by social stigma. All of this is to the detriment of the individual trying to simply gain an education in university.

Some people argue that college is still worth it because you learn about yourself in college and you grow as a person through the many activities. Proponents argue that you can have fun in college and make long-lasting memories and friendships. However, this can easily be done outside of college for free, and it is difficult to grow as a person in college. What do I mean by this? You grow as a person when you are challenged and then overcome such challenges. As described before, the academic standards of colleges are so low that they will never actually fail out a student. Why? It is because each student is a cash cow paying the university thousands of dollars through student loans. For personal growth, you need the possibility of failure. When students take these nonchallenging courses and majors like gender studies, communications, or broadcast journalism, it is not allowing them to grow because they are not challenged. Also, it is information that can easily be learned online, and it will not provide large returns to offset the loans after graduation.

One of the most ludicrous classes I took during my time in college was University 101. It was a three-credit hour course designed for freshmen to assist with their transition into college, and I was pressured by the university to attend the class. It was an absolute waste of money and time where I learned nothing useful. Besides learning nothing, the slot took away from other classes I could have taken to graduate even faster. During the course, the professor would simply go over university rules and procedures. He would sometimes throw in some interesting facts about the school's history. There would be an unproductive class debate occasionally that led to me getting lampooned by other students for my conservative beliefs of gun ownership. Following that specific class, another conservative came up to me and said he agreed with me but did not want to speak up because of fear of repercussions and the liberal mob in the class. There was a peer leader with the class who taught with the professor, however, on one occasion the professor intentionally did not come to class, so the peer leader could talk about drinking and other aspects of partying. We were all significantly under aged in the class. It was a prime example of the drinking and partying culture on campus, and the class furthered that culture. There are innumerable examples of other courses like this that do not belong in the college curriculum. They do not add to the overall degree programs, and more importantly, the information can be found online. These classes waste the student's time and money.

Entire majors in college now are complete nonsense, and almost all the information can be learned through online classes. However, do not dare take college classes online because it will cost the same price per credit as an in-person class, which boggles my mind. What are you paying for when you take an online course from the university? Sometimes, universities charge more for online classes.[84] The university, in a fundamental sense of the word, is moving to the internet on platforms like YouTube, where lectures are given for free and knowledge can be gained. But, the classical university, if it were to wholly move to an online version, there would be no one that would reasonably want to attend. Why would anyone pay so much for online courses while the same information can be learned for free or through websites like Skillshare or Masterclasses. Alongside dumb majors and courses are programs just designed to attract students to the university. During my time in college, I was a part of one of these programs called Capstone Scholars. It was simply an organization to group students together with great extracurriculars in high school. It did not do anything beneficial to the overall pursuit of knowledge, and it was a complete waste of time and money even though it would provide the occasional scholarship.

The idea of who should attend university is a cost benefit analysis. Certainly, those who receive massive scholarships to attend university have a better chance at receiving a positive return on investment. These people who are very academically inclined, providing a great benefit to the university, should strongly consider university even though there are other failures with higher education. They will have to deal with everything from the drinking culture to postmodern indoctrination, but there is very little cost if everything is paid for in the long run. For those who are required to attend university and aim to become STEM field experts, doctors, or lawyers, there are several ways that a full ride might be obtained. One of the most apparent is to be intellectually inclined where the university gives a scholarship based on superb grades and test scores. Another way is to utilize a talent in a sport to get a scholarship for playing that sport at a collegiate level. Further, the military gives out scholarships to those who would pledge to serve a specific branch for a designated period of time either in active or reserve status. These are all great ways to pay for higher education if you actually need to attend university, and there are many more options for those that investigate further scholarships.

Some people need to go to college. However, a significant amount of these graduates leave college and are now doing jobs that did not require degrees in previous generations. But now they have a diploma. They are college educated. Will it be worth the 20 years of perpetual servitude to these loans when the education could have been earned online? In the increasingly abundant world of the internet many people are beginning to argue that universities have no benefit besides accreditation. Although this is increasingly true, some university majors need the skills from that teaching in order to progress in their specific career field, even though this too is moving more online. These majors essentially use university as a trade school, and these are generally the majors in the STEM fields. Many of the other problems within higher education still apply to these majors, but the cost to benefit for these majors is much different than others, and I think that there may be a movement in these classes to an online structure just further in the future than the humanities.

Chapter XIII

Follow Opportunity, Not Passion

"We often miss opportunity because it's dressed in overalls and looks like work." —Thomas A. Edison

N ever give up on your dreams. Do what you have a passion for. Never let anyone tell you differently or bring you down. Because you can do it! These are the classic clichés told to many young people as they develop through their teens and early twenties. But do the people who declare these subjective announcements even know your dreams? Do they know where your dream will lead you? I am fully on board with the idea of dedication as one of the fundamentals to success, but, sometimes your skill set and passion do not even remotely align.[85] Just because you are passionate about a particular subject does not mean that you will be good at that subject. Nor does it mean that if you pursue such a passion it will produce a career for you to engage with. Passions are important, and you should take them along for whatever career you pursue, but do not let them control your career decisions if you are terrible at that passion. Generally, passions lead to hobbies that are a celebrated aspect of normal life, but they usually do not coincide with your more productive skill set for other opportunities. If you work on your passion, you will probably progress at it, but that does not mean that you should make it a job when other profitable opportunities are around that are a better match with your particular skills.

Another problem with universities is that they force this mentality of following what you are passionate about regardless of what you are good at with your individual skill set. Students who have little skills in singing, dancing, or art will go to college and earn a degree in these things even though they would do far better to follow opportunities that better match their skill set. Unless you sing like Amy Winehouse or paint like Michelangelo, your major should not be in those fields, and it is not worth paying all that money for which you can do it online for free. Those passions of art or dance or film studies can be hobbies. They are not going to really serve you in the long run if you do not have the requisite skill set or the ability to create the skill set for a field to do well. Many university students have this idea of the dream job. But, usually, it will be just that, a dream. Moreover, this artificial idea of the dream job can cloud your view of other opportunities. The movie *The Pursuit of Happiness* illustrates this idea of following opportunity. The main character might have had the passion to sell medical devices in the past, but he quickly realized that the opportunity shifted in the market for his passion. He was far better at using his skill set on Wall Street, which was the opportunity he eventually found. The realities of the current job market, especially in 2020, point to the idea that people should look where everyone is going and do the opposite. Millions of jobs are going unfilled because of the skills gap, and there is a massive amount of opportunity out there that is beyond the view of your passion.

Follow Opportunity, Not Passion

At one time in my life, I was extremely passionate about football, however, I quickly realized how horrible I was at the sport. I was not cut out for it in many respects, but I found that my skills were better suited for running. I found the opportunity outside of football and began to excel at it even though I was not passionate about it at first. If I were to continue to focus on football, I would have never been able to find other things to focus on that I was better at. Many of my friends like to play basketball, but they are not seven feet tall, nor can they dunk like Lebron James. It would be unwise for them to continue in the sport and to see it as a possible career. It is great for them to keep it as a passion and hobby, but not to follow it as a career. From a young age, and even until today, I am passionate about exercising and living a clean lifestyle, but I recognize that being a fitness model, nutritionist, or personal trainer is not for me because my skill set would be better exploited in another field. I am following opportunity rather than my passion. I am following the opportunity where I believe my skill set will be utilized to make the collective of human existence just a little bit better, and I think it would be wise for university students to reflect on their passions and skill sets. Differentiate between the two and make rational decisions going forward. For some lucky people, their skills and passions align. If so, that is amazing. But, for a lot of people, they absolutely do not.

Many students come into college with the idea of finding themselves. They have undeclared majors and mess around for months on courses that might not even add to their overall career. They engage in other failures of college through their lack of focus, like partying and doing the bare minimum in classes. If this is your mentality, do not go to college. It is a waste of your time and money. Without a solid game plan before you enter, you are setting yourself up for failure. Getting rid of undeclared majors is one-way universities could encourage people who do not have a plan to not attend. If you do not know what you want to do when you go into college or at least have an idea of something you want to do and a plan to accomplish it, then take a gap year working or interning so you can figure it out. You will be able to save more time and money by taking this time to focus on your life goals and finding your skill set for your future career.

There are some fields in which the college diploma is necessary. Most are professional degrees for careers in engineering, mathematics, science, technology, medicine, or law. Because you need the required knowledge for these professions, it is necessary to get a diploma for acceptance into these fields or graduate institutions. There are still most of the problems with undergrad that one must deal with before moving on into the professional career like the gen-ed requirements. There are programs that would combine medical school with an undergraduate degree into a six-year program. The same is being considered for law school, as well. These ideas are helpful and should be radically expanded, or the accreditation needs to shift from requiring a university degree in these programs to just requiring a test of requisite knowledge before entering the professional school. There could be much cheaper studying tools used for this, and self-studying would be the key factor in determining whether someone progresses into that professional school. It is peculiar that, with law school specifically, one is required to gain an undergraduate degree of a type that will not be utilized in law school itself. It is possible that types of law might coincide with the undergraduate major, but there are no required classes for law school, so it seems foolish to require a degree that only marginally adds to the overall atmosphere of law school.

The people who are benefiting from college are overwhelmingly the colleges themselves as they are classified as 501(c)(3) organizations, which do not have to pay taxes. Sporting event tickets, concert tickets, tuition, donations, income from investments, all of it is tax exempt. Public and private universities can gain this status, which is odd as one would expect only the public universities to have this privilege. The modern university is a massive business, wealthier than many countries, and their endowments could pay the university tuition of students for decades, sometimes even centuries, into the future. Technology has made everything faster and cheaper, but college takes the same amount of time for most students, and it costs just the same. There are several shady aspects that have caused tuition to rise in recent decades, but reason is the greed of the political elite. Board members—many of which are political donors—rarely reflect the will of the students or the faculty, so it is difficult to have accurate representative change in the university system. The board sometimes doles out favors for campus business to the lowest bidder. Because the entire campus can be monetized through contracts for construction, food, disposal, and cleaning, it allows for the board to control massive amounts of money that is ripe for corruption.

Higher education also has a monopoly on an athletic system where young athletes bring in millions of dollars to the university system yet do not get paid. This is slowly changing as the NCAA is beginning to get more pressure to let college athletes get paid for their work. The original idea was that athletes were getting paid with an education, which is absurd, especially when these athletes move into the professional leagues. The value of the education they gain is dependent on the universities actually providing some sense of value, but the modern university does not provide this as the access to information has so radically increased. Therefore, it is erroneous to say that athletes are getting paid through free education because that education is almost worthless, and it is especially dependent on the brand name of the school. Sadly, university is becoming more and more of a credential, and it matters to employers where the student went to school. It is not about the education they received at the school, but whether it is a brand name school. This demonstrates that the idea of college is not about education anymore. It is a credential and accreditation service that provides information to employers on whether you can pass through an arbitrary selection process that favors certain minorities and the rich, a perversion of what university should be about. Students must realize this and decide whether university is actually the right choice regardless of athletic scholarship. They must follow the opportunities where they lie even if they are outside of college or even outside of sports.

Part Three

Personal Trials

Chapter XIV

High School and Family Experience

"The homemaker has the ultimate career. All other careers exist for one purpose only—and that is to support the ultimate career."—C.S. Lewis

I was extremely blessed in my education during high school, attending a small private Catholic school in Middle Tennessee. This school was able to craft and mold me into the person I am today, and I see my high school experience as the roots of my education. A good education lasts forever was the mantra of the school, and it is a motto I have implemented, expanding my wisdom daily through books and documentaries.

At the beginning of my high school experience, I was not academically inclined and did not apply myself as much as I could have. My freshman year was marred by indifference towards academics, as I focused on my lackluster performance on the football team. I was far more passionate about the sport than grades or other activities. But as the season dragged on—we finished the season with a 1-9 record—I began to realize that football might not be in my future because I was horrible at it. Around the same time, I was having trouble in my Latin class. I was sliding by with average grades in every other class, but Latin was especially challenging. My teacher forcing me to come to office hours to study was the watershed moment when I realized that if I applied my skills to studying then I could do exceptionally well. This realization and discovery of my potential came at the end of the year, but the mentality carried over into the next years as I dropped football and continued to engage in academics. To my Latin teacher, who took the time to help me discover what I was good and passionate about, I owe a debt of gratitude for what I am today. I thank her for the encouragement and guidance she provided for my journey through life.

I focused on nothing but the course material, and I noticed that I was good at retaining knowledge if I studied. This skill would eventually develop into a passion of learning for the sake of learning. During my sophomore year, I achieved straight As in all my classes. Even though they were all regular classes, I was able to do exceptionally well. I would get more than a perfect score on many of my tests, especially in general chemistry where I had multiple high achieving accomplishments. I was able to progress into all advanced classes and two AP courses the next year, where I would be pressured to start my journey to begin building my resume for college. My grades were on point during my junior year, but in one interaction with another influential teacher, I was persuaded that grades were not enough for college. I wanted to go to college because I wanted to learn more as I had a skill set within me and a potential for gaining more knowledge. So, I had to join extracurriculars. I became hyper focused on everything that would lead me into college from jumping into two AP courses to joining clubs. Before this I was never in any clubs or activities besides football.

Annoyingly, I established my own club called the Fitness Club, where I would get a group of friends together during the lunch period to simply talk about lifting weights and exercise. Even though I enjoyed it thoroughly, it was purely for the resume I was trying to build for college, as I was under the impression that only the best extracurriculars would allow me to attend a prestigious university. I ran for student body president during this time, and it was abundantly clear to the rest of my class that I was just trying to pad my resume. Though I was able to gain the support of the lower classmen and win the election, I was not doing it out of the goodness of my heart to help the school. The president had no power, anyway, so being elected did really matter in itself. I joined every single club I could think of including Model UN, Science Olympiad, Youth in Government, and the Math club. I emphatically embraced the idea of becoming a Renaissance man. During my senior year, I would eventually drop most of the activities, especially those that did not matter after college applications were submitted. I pushed further academically during my senior year to take five AP courses along with theology and advanced pre-calculus. One of the things I did to boost my resume in the summer before senior year was enrolling into dual enrollment courses in a community college near my home. The twelve credit hours I took were exclusively online in the studies of sociology, psychology, American history, and public speaking. These were relatively easy courses, and you got out of them what you put into them. And, this was my first taste of how college could be vastly streamlined. Even though I did not plan for these courses to help me graduate college quickly, they were useful, along with AP credit, in providing a way to get out of wasting my time in the general education requirements of the universities. Sometimes there are scholarships for these dual enrollment courses, depending on the student's grade, and I would have been eligible if I had made the deadline. So, it is important for high schools and parents to supervise students and dates for scholarships and applications as dual enrollment can be very beneficial later down the line.

At the same time, I spent that entire summer studying for the ACT, which was a semi-useless endeavor. I learned the entire set of grammar rules set out by the test, which has continued to help me over the years, but I spent too much time on things like high-level mathematics. The ACT might need to reform itself as colleges get rid of general education requirements. The ACT could take on a different form where the test is focused on subject matter that relates to the students intended major, and then the colleges accept students for a major based on the focused ACT. Moreover, high schools should not indoctrinate students with the social pressure of attending college by promoting standardized testing. Students in their freshmen or sophomore year are usually required to take the PSAT, but it should not be pushed on those who are not going to attend college and could make a great career in a vocational setting. That social pressure and the creation of a sunk-cost fallacy is what drives thousands of high school students to college, the idea that it is expected of them since the beginning of high school. Instead of looking for other opportunities, they were clouded by the stigma of not attending college, even though it might not be the right thing for them.

High School and Family Experience

The college admissions process ramped up during my senior year when I began working on applications. I applied to too many universities; and it was a failure of the high school to not discourage me from doing this because I spread myself too thin and wasted money in the process. It was the most stressful and emotionally disturbing time during high school, as I was rejected from every so-called "prestigious" university. In hindsight, this was a miracle because I would avoid the arbitrary rules of some universities that do not accept AP classes or limit how early one can graduate. Not attending a private name brand university just because of a name and the understanding that it would be a ticket to success also saved me thousands of dollars. I have come to realize how little the name brand of the school factors into an individual's success, so I would have relaxed more if I knew that grit was more important than the name of the school. I felt this way because of the major social pressure I was under from the stigma of not attending college and my peers who were getting into universities like Columbia, Yale, or Washington University. However, this is one of the aspects in high school that should change as we move away from the pressure for all students to go to college and as the university fundamentally moves more online.

Although I understand that many people do not have the same opportunity across the United States in terms of high school education, there needs to be greater focus on the development of the student in high school. This is especially the case when high schools send their students into the flawed higher education system. As with college, there are more and more opportunities to gain education from an online source. They are even accredited by the state in some situations.[86]

During summers, parents should investigate enrolling their children in these programs. One can study for AP tests outside the classroom during their free time. The summer provides a great opportunity for high school students to work on these courses to get college credit if their schools do not provide AP courses in the curriculum.[87] Students can do dual enrollment, but there is usually a higher price on this than AP courses. Sometimes there are scholarships associated with dual enrollment at the nearest community college. High school is a paramount time to develop students into scholars.

There needs to be, at least, a two-path mentality with a different focus on each. There needs to be a college path in which high school students are provided with all the material necessary to get through college as soon as possible in the least expensive way with a game plan. There needs to be another path in preparing students who do not attend college. This program will illustrate some of the major, post-high school opportunities associated with vocational skills. This will give students more opportunities besides college, so they do not feel pressure to attend college since attending one is surely not a guarantee of success.

During the summers for the college track, students need to be taught basic courses like psychology and sociology, and high schools need to take on the responsibility of having the general education requirements of college met. During the summers for the career track, internships or apprenticeships need to be fully utilized for students to find a vocation suitable to their skills. Along with college fairs in the high school, there needs to be vocational school or trade school fairs where those who do not want to attend university go to find internships.

High School and Family Experience

A lot of the success of a student comes from his or her family, where parents can set goals with the child and ensure academic progress through monitoring grades. Parents must promote the role of education in the student's world. The best predictor of student success is the extent to which parents and family culture emphasize and involve themselves in the child's education.[88] Before we can have a discussion on the policy changes that state governments can make in order to emphasize high school education and establish better education, parents must take greater personal responsibility to take every opportunity to promote education in the household. This is especially the case in single parent households, which generally provide less opportunity for children to engage in education, so the parents need to really focus on the education of the child.[89] Reading books or the newspaper is a great way for parents to start setting a strong example for children. Actively involving yourself in the education of your child inside and outside the school is another great way to show children the importance of education. Cultures emphasizing learning in the household partly explains why some cultures have more academic success than others.

My father taught me discipline through a military style upbringing. I had room checks for cleanliness and continual oversight of many aspects of my education. I developed the fundamentals of hard work from my mother who continually amazed me by running her own chiropractic practice with the highest efficiency. My sister taught me two aspects relating to education: the importance of competition and what not to do when entering college. Because my sister is older, she has been the guinea pig who can impart knowledge and wisdom to me. We have always been competitive, and it has driven me to accomplish many things. More importantly, I learned from her that if you do not enter college with a game plan or decide to shift course in college you will not be able to graduate with efficiency, and you will have a far more difficult time as you take on more loans. I learned many of the things I should avoid in college through my sister, and many of the aspects of the failures of the university system were avoided because of her experience. Hopefully, this book will help you avoid the errors of those who have gone before you in college.

Chapter XV

Memoirs of a College Student

"No one can construct for you the bridge upon which precisely you must cross the stream of life, no one but you yourself alone."
—Friedrich Nietzsche

When I got all my college acceptances during the spring of my senior year of high school, I had to decide which school to choose. The high school advisors and my parents recommended that I choose the university that I felt most comfortable at. They also stressed that the name of the school was an important factor. I narrowed it down to either going to a small private school in California, where my sister was attending, or a couple southern universities. I took a trip to Malibu, California and realized that the atmosphere there was not one where I would thrive in, although the cost compared to my other options was significantly less. Even though it was a high-ranked school on paper, it would cost me tens of thousands of dollars more. My options were limited to two southern schools in South Carolina, one public and one private. I compared the costs and relative programs for my desired major, and I toured each school to make sure I would be comfortable. I was deciding against bitter rivals, but I simply went off the cost comparison, strength of the political science program, and the overall comfort I felt there. I chose to go to the public university in the heart of South Carolina.

I enjoyed my college experience. It was a time of tremendous growth, both personally, physically, and mentally. There were just major issues that I witnessed at my time in the higher education system that were the same ones happening across the nation. The university I attended is not the only university suffering from the problems listed above. It is the failure of the entire education system that is setting up students to fail in the real world after graduation. My personal anecdotes are here to represent a microcosm of the problems with higher education.

Before students even begin to take courses at the university, they are subjected to college orientation, where they are instructed on common sense principles like the criminality of assault or the prohibition of cheating. But how much do students remember from these sessions? I certainly do not remember everything besides the overall outline of what was discussed, like the health center and student success center. The one thing I vividly remember was how the orientation treated us like children, as though we were completely ignorant of the wrongfulness of sexually assaulting someone or the unauthorized consumption of alcohol. Further, the orientation never taught us about hookup culture, the consequences of frequent sexual activity, or ever tried to discourage under aged drinking. The orientation staff addressed only the problems that were a consequence of frequent hooking up. They assumed that everyone would partake in drinking alcohol, so they told us how to do it safely.

Memoirs of a College Student

The practical aspects of getting your schedule on point and making sure you know where the student health center could easily be done on the internet. Moreover, the commonsense advice of not sexually assaulting women and doing dumb things while drinking alcohol are just that: common sense. The family should already have infused the child going into the school with the requisite morality to not commit such offenses. That is why it is vital for the family to be at the forefront of education, and it is why proper care in raising a child is so important.

Following orientation, there were a few weeks before I would begin taking classes at the university, but, oddly, freshmen were barred from taking summer courses before entering in the fall. It was my desire to hit the ground running in the summer, but the university made sure all the incoming students were new to the campus and college. In hindsight, I should have taken community college classes during that summer to further my advance through undergrad. Nonetheless, I was just beginning to feel the frustration with the system of higher education. In the middle of August, I was moved into the dormitories that would be my residence for the year. The university required all freshmen to live on campus, which felt like a usurpation of my liberty. If someone wants to live off campus for any reason, they should be able to do so. The university should not force students to pay for their overpriced room and board and be stuck in a place with students they do not like and overseen by a resident assistants who is only marginally older but wields power. I did not start classes immediately, yet we were brought to the university early to bond in freshmen activities on the campus, like those done on a high school field day. This was the so-called first night in Carolina where students were grouped together to play games, eat food, and listen to music. This was all mandatory fun. The resident assistants forced the students to attend. I was not able to simply sit in my room and read a book or study for upcoming classes. Instead, I had to play around and stand in the middle of campus to placate others who put on the event. The consensus of my cohorts at the university was that it was a waste of their time and one of the most awkward periods of their college experience. This type of ceremony where freshmen students are grouped together for supposedly fun activities and food is one seen on most campuses across the nation. The universities need to find their roots. They need to understand what is essential and what is fluff. They are acting more like a business, providing an experience rather than an educational center of knowledge. I wanted to become educated, not play cornhole while music was being blasted in the center of campus. University is not a big party; it should be there for education. Because this education is leaving university and moving online, the administrators want to provide that experience as a replacement. If they did not, college students might actually realize that higher education is not worth it anymore.

The university forces most incoming college freshmen to live on campus during their first year, some even dictating mandatory residence for two or more years while they take classes. They claim this requirement for the protection of students and for the purpose of making friendships. However, I was more annoyed than friendly with my dorm neighbors. The dorm floor students were immature. Their living habits were outside of the realm of conduct for a normal adult, and they would party late into the night, not adhering to the overall rules of the building. Participating in illegal activities, they would harass me as I simply tried to read or study. Even though my roommate and suitemates were great companions, most of the other students on the dorm floor were very immature. Further, this type of housing allows students to become distracted rather than focusing wholeheartedly on academics. Possibly, the grouping of young students could be beneficial for study sessions among students. However, the university does not put students into dorm buildings based on major, and study groups are not exclusive to places where students live. Study groups can meet anywhere, and they do not have to live together. From my experience, this requirement breeds more distractions than an intellectual community striving for a pursuit of knowledge. I could see a benefit for living on campus if the university were to set up buildings for specific majors where all the students are going through the same classes, so there could be more of an intellectual atmosphere. However, the university moving online will eradicate the need for dorm building, so this issue will soon disappear. Regardless, the university should not assume that every student coming into higher education is not able to take care of themselves in the most basic manner. The university should not dictate the living condition of the students, especially when they overcharge for the room and board.

During the first semester, I was required to fulfill the core requirements of my degree, and so I had to sign up for basic English, calculus, history, and Spanish courses. As I, a political science major, sat in calculus class wondering what the hell derivatives had to do with anything remotely related to my field of study I began questioning the institution of college. The simple answer is that it did not have anything to do with it, and it was bureaucratic formality that I had to check the box of completed core requirements. But it is not just checking a box, and many students do not realize the cost of checking that box until it is too late. Those classes that had nothing to do with my major cost me tens of thousands of dollars and wasted valuable time early in my life when I could have been focusing elsewhere for more productivity. I have heard arguments that taking the core classes gives students a wide breadth of knowledge, but I do not want to pay thousands of dollars for information I could gain for free online. Furthermore, I was in my English class where the focus was on the feminist leaders throughout the history of literature, which is an interesting topic, but we slightly touched the topics of grammar, syntax, or even persuasive arguments. A tangential course that was taught was one on learning English through satire, which sounds interesting on paper; however, most of the course was just watching satire and writing about it. Thankfully, I only had to take a couple more core class requirements in the coming semesters. Taking those classes was an utter waste of time and money. I could have learned the information for free online and gained more from that source than the college class.

Throughout my college experience, I tried only marginally in most of my classes, skipping the readings in favor of my own non-fiction tastes. Knowing I wanted to enter law school, where my undergrad degree would essentially be worthless, I did not have the requisite motivation to actively try hard in the courses. Even then, I was able to get an A in most of my courses because I would show up to every class. Though I did not usually read the assignments, I would still try to learn everything I could during classes. But, when I would go into class, I would be surrounded with students who looked like they hated their lives. I saw faces of indifference, which did not seem to care about the pursuit of knowledge. Students would come in late, disrupting the entire class, and causing everyone to lose focus. Some students would not even show up to class and try to get the notes from other students. The professors seem engaged in the material, and I have had some wonderful professors in political science and history. But some of the professors do not focus on teaching because they are more concerned about doing their research, so it added to the atmosphere of apathy in these classes. As noted earlier, students are doing significantly less work than past generations. There are multiple examples that come to mind when thinking about this. For example, the professor in one of my political science classes asked a question on the reading assignment. There was dead silence from the 50 students. Granted, I added to the problem by also not reading, but the point that there is high student apathy is true. This happened repeatedly throughout my classes, and my colleagues have concurred on the subject that there is low student engagement in most courses. Now, there are lively student interactions in some classes with great professors that even engage apathetic students, but they are becoming few and far between.

Even before entering the gilded gates of university, I had the presumption that alcohol would be an aspect of the college experience for many people, but I never expected it to be such a major element in the system. I was the only person who I encountered in my entire time at college who did not partake in drinking alcohol. There was a pervading atmosphere of partying and drinking, especially when it came to gamedays. It was a common occurrence for hundreds of students to go downtown throughout the week even when they had class the next day. It is like these students who party and engage in that conduct do not have the foresight to think a couple years into the future where their present actions have great importance. If you see the future as important, then all that occurs in the present is important. Things build off each other, and partying, drinking, and illegal conduct are like building your future on sand. There was one time where I was outside on a Friday night, and I saw a truck with about 10 people inside it and in the trunk, screaming and being negligent. Further, I saw people when I went out for my morning runs, at five in the morning, returning from the bars from the night before, stumbling around and trying to get back to the dorm. The resident advisors are barely any help in that they participate in the same sort of conduct, and they are only marginally more mature than the students. Students would throw parties in their own dorm rooms, drinking alcohol with the resident advisors. Therefore, there needs to be a crackdown on this sort of conduct because it does not enhance the purpose of the university. It arguably degrades the purpose of university.

Another part of my college experience was the hookup culture, where sexual norms were essentially disregarded, especially when it came to drinking alcohol. I would have conversations with students who discussed their recent hookups as though they were seeking glory through them or wanting praise for completing a remarkable endeavor. Many would detest the slightest thought of having a monogamous relationship, instead absorbed in the idea that the friends with benefits title was their forte. They disdain having feelings for the other person they were hooking up with, like it was a disease, and they decoupled the action of hooking up with the emotional and physical consequences of it. Many have argued that it is empowering women, and that there is a double standard for men and women in this society. They are fighting the wretched patriarchy, they claim. But, as the statistics have displayed before, the double standard that existed in the past is generally gone, and men and women are engaging in this conduct generally at the same rates. I do not see engaging in repeated sexual conduct as an empowering act for women just as I do not see it as empowering for men. There are serious societal, emotional, and physical problems that come with decoupling sexual conduct with its consequences.

During the first year of college, I would usually wake up around 4 in the morning to get a run in before going to the ROTC training, so I would go outside to the study room to not disturb my roommate. But this time the door to the study room was closed, which was odd. I opened the door to my horror to find students engaging in sexual conduct in the dark. It scared the hell out of me. The room is for studying and not that sort of behavior. They eventually left, but that was the starkest example of how the life of a college student is dominated by hookup culture. Throughout most of my time in university, I was socially ostracized for openly engaging in this behavior. It was frowned upon because of the social pressure to engage in hookup culture. The solution to this is that students need to voluntarily set better examples for others when it comes to having sexual relationships. Both men and women need to hold a higher standard that does not include frequent one-night stands with people you have only just recently met.

Throughout my time in college classes, it was an ever-apparent aspect of my humanities courses that there was a leftist lean to the teaching of Western history and some political commentary. It was most apparent in my European history class, where the professors seemed to disdain the West and openly promoted socialism in the class. Only one brave soul to my right raised his hand to confront the professor on the ideas of socialism. But it did not really matter too much because many students hold their professors in such a high regard that they trust anything they say. I encountered another professor like this in another class about civil rights where the professor would posit the idea that many are now beginning to maintain that America writ large is a racist society. No one would argue with the professor on the good things that America has done. Instead, the students would simply agree for the better grade and passively accept what the professors teach without any skepticism. A more moderate class was taught by an eight-year-old professor, who was a strong Democrat in the region. Even though he was firmly on the left, he did not try to indoctrinate his students, but just imparted his wisdom of the political system to the students. I greatly appreciated this. Professor's purpose should be to impart this wisdom to their students instead of trying to indoctrinate them with a particular ideology.

The safe space culture on campus was also very apparent as there were frequent demonstrations protesting "hate speech" and lack of racial or ethnic diversity. Many students simply did not believe in free speech, believing some speech was violence and some speech could only occur in specific zones of free speech. Students would end conversations with me the moment things got upsetting to them. They intellectually collapsed and mentally recused themselves out of fear of being triggered. I would be having a discussion on a relatively controversial topic with other students, but they get very emotional to which they end the conversation. This is not the point of college. Universities need to promote free speech and the open discussion of ideas, so student do not collapse at the slightest nonconforming opinion. Leftist students would silence anything remotely on the right side of the political spectrum by saying it was racist or sexist. They label others as either sexist, racist, or classist in order to not have to deal with the arguments they are proposing. It is a way to end conversations, so their fragile worldview might not be imposed on by countervailing conservative ideas. The idea is that if someone is labeled racist or sexist then someone does not have to intellectually debate with that person. It is a way to shut down free speech and debate. Critical thinking and productive debates go out the window with this ideology reigning supreme, and I have seen it as a growing trend on campuses in just the past two years. Safe spaces that silence particular speech is a slippery slope that leads to the absolute limitation of free speech, antithetical to the pursuit of human wisdom that should characterize university.

Another thing I noticed during my time in college was an example of college students lacking personal responsibility. It was the rumored "freshman fifteen," a saying attributed to the idea that students cannot control their eating habits and overindulge in their meal plans. Even though there are students lacking food in college, a significant portion of the college freshman class overeat with their meal plans. There are healthy options to eat from, but many students, away from their parents, are postponing adulthood, where they must be healthy, and decide to eat horrible foods. At the gym there would be an influx of students at the beginning of each semester, but the numbers would dramatically taper off as the semester dragged on. Most students have the time to be healthy, but they do not take the responsibility to do so, gaining the "freshman fifteen." Students need to take radical personal responsibility in every aspect of their lives, moving forward proudly and expeditiously into maturity. One time, a friend of mine seemed sad, so I asked her what was wrong. She said that she was upset that the school year was ending because she would have to go back home where there were rules. It is this mentality that demonstrates how little responsibility college students adopt in their personal lives, and it displays the idea that colleges are now just where people go to prolong infancy rather than progressing into maturity.

Many of my fellow students complained about their student loan debt, and it was a comedic trope to reference the debt during class discussion or other times during college activities. They acted like they were not going to have to eventually pay it back, like it was not real. But this debt is real, and it kicks graduates in the teeth when they receive their diploma. Many students in college were just prolonging adolescence, not knowing that taxes exist or having any clue as to their post-graduation employment opportunities. It was Neverland for students, and when I would ask them about their debt or paying it back, they would say that it will be easy or that it is a problem for their future selves. I would further ask what they think they will make when they exit college, and most replied with salaries ranging from seventy thousand to one hundred and twenty thousand dollars. A disconnect with college students exists, one where they think they will exit college with a job tied with a nice bow and served on a silver platter at a salary of their choosing. This is certainly not the case, and it is going to get worse as students do not grow up and get their decisions under control. They need to realize how important every decision is to the future and that no one will be there to help them when they are down. Adolescence should not be prolonged. These college students need to know the ramifications of taking on student loans and having to be an adult. The universities of today are not setting up an environment where students can enter adulthood. Low academic standards, a partying and hookup culture, and a lack of personal responsibility have combined to create the perfect environment to fail thousands of graduates by holding them in immaturity.

Chapter XVI

Insider Information

"I'm so fast that last night I turned off the light switch in my hotel room and was in bed before the room was dark."
—Muhammad Ali

Why would you want to go through university quickly? Why wouldn't you want to take it all in and make some great memories? Aren't you going to miss out on the college experience? The instant I began making my game plan to graduate in two years before entering college I was repeatedly asked by my fellow students the above questions. I just stopped answering them or usually just replied with a simple "Because." But there were many reasons that I wanted to get out of college as soon as possible. The first reason is the problematic culture of college from the partying and hooking up to the drinking and academic apathy. I desired a Type A environment, and in undergrad those types of personalities are few and far between. Another reason was that it costs thousands of dollars for this education, and it is not wise to waste time when that time is so valuable. Many students simply put it in the back of their mind that they are spending thousands of dollars and do not think about having to pay it back until they graduate. I have heard the mantra that "college is only once but you'll work for the rest of your life."

INTRO TO FAILURE

This is an abhorrent ideology to live by in which one abstains from responsibility while staying in a state of prolonged adolescence. This is not good for students, their family, their community, the university, or the country. It is seriously wrong that we have a culture on campus that promotes this idea of prolonged adolescence. College students need to grow up. Another reason why I wanted to graduate so quickly is because everything in life is a race. Those who are most successful are usually the first to do something. So, I realized that it was imperative to move quickly and save time and money while going through college. I wanted to become a lawyer and head into law school, where my undergraduate degree would be almost entirely meaningless, so I had a major incentive to go as quickly as possible.

During one of my first year advising sessions, I laid out the plan to my advisor to which she responded with disapproval, asking me the questions everyone had asked me before. Why not spend more time in college? I told her I do not like to waste time. She then told me that it was not possible. However, I had done the math, adding up the credit. I had been planning this for months, detailing every aspect of my progression. I knew she was wrong. I had to schedule another meeting to get everything straightened out, and this was one of the times where I noticed the inefficiencies of the higher education system caused by administrative bloat. This "advisor" just showed me how to navigate a website and criticized my plan to graduate early. There was no new information she imparted to me through the process.

If you actually still plan on attending college because it is a required part of your particular career or you have a good scholarship or just need to get through it efficiently for some other reason, there are multiple ways that I leveraged the higher education system to work for my benefit. First, there are several colleges, mainly private schools, that will limit the time in which you can graduate from the university. Usually, they will cap the time at around three years. But there are those universities, mainly public state schools, that will allow students to graduate in only two years. Universities that accept credits from other sources, and do not expressly limit the time when you graduate, will be the best universities to attend for the purpose of finishing early. It happened by chance that I chose a university that would accept the credits I already had and did not actually limit the time of graduation. I realized this when I was planning to graduate early right before entering higher education. Overall, most public colleges will be the best bet for those students wanting to graduate in an extremely efficient manner.

Once you have chosen the school that will offer the best opportunity when it comes to graduating quickly, the work must be done during high school for you to accomplish this. The AP credit test must have been taken during high school and dual enrollment must have been taken before entering college. Some of my friends in college are graduating in three years total, and they could have done it in two years if they just had more AP, IB, or dual enrollment credits. So, these factors will make it much easier to move quickly through university. The key is to do well on these exams, so the university will accept them. Even if your high school does not offer AP credit, you can still study for the test and take it to try and get the college credit. Some high schools offer IB courses, which essentially do the same as AP courses. Utilize all these credits to get out of the courses that are a part of the general education requirements of the university. If you have any dual enrollment credits, those will be helpful, as well. The summer before college can be used to study and take CLEP exams, where you can get out of some of the general education courses. Placing out of the foreign language requirements will also be a big help, so make sure you study for the incoming freshman language assessment. Even if you did not take any applicable language in high school, use the summer to study a language intensely before taking the exam so you can get out of it.

Say, for example, you did not have the opportunity to take AP credit or dual enrollment before entering college. One of the first things you could do is overload your schedule to eighteen credit hours instead of fifteen, even though academic advisors claim that it will be much more difficult than a regular class schedule. But this largely depends on your major. I took overloaded schedules before and did not find it that much more difficult. Whether it is difficult will depend on the specific university you attend as well. At state schools and outside the STEM fields, it should be only marginally more difficult to overload your schedule. A caveat to this is if you must work while taking classes, which will make things a bit more difficult. But working around an extra class should not be that much more difficult. Sometimes paid internships are offered to students in a major in the surrounding areas of campus, and sometimes you can get credit for that internship. Universities should expand programs like these or even make work experience satisfy some of the general education requirements.

One of the best times during my college experience was summer classes, where I took twelve credits during the summer between my first and second year. The class sizes were small, so I was able to talk to my professors and engage with the material. Most of the students were still apathetic to the whole process, but it was very engaging. There was almost no one on campus, so it was very refreshing to be relatively alone. The courses were streamlined, and two of them were only for three weeks. This is when I realized that the information in college courses is not particularly special and that you could find it online. I only had to write a single paper and show up to the class to receive an A, so the academic standards were quite low. Some students still did not show up to class, even though the entire course was only three weeks. By having courses like this in the summer, with low academic standards and little information to impart, the university is allowing students to simply just check a box. This was another time where I intensely began to question the actual value of college and the dilemma of how online information competes with the accreditation of higher education.

One of the most important things when attending university is having your major already planned out because changing it mid-way through your upper level courses will put you behind. So, pick a major where you know you will succeed with your skill set. Some majors have more required courses, so moving quickly through those majors might not be the best thing, especially if you go into that field right after college. This is regarding the STEM fields, where the university is essentially acting as a trade school and teaching you the skills that you will need in that field. Usually, STEM fields will have many more requirements for the degree itself, so it may be more challenging to graduate early. I still recommend that you utilize summer courses to get out of the general education requirements, which will still apply to STEM majors. Some majors will also require a minor or cognate, and I recommend going with the one that makes you take the least amount of credits because the minor or cognate will help very little in the long run and the material will probably be better learned online for a lower price. If you double major, it will take far longer to graduate than one who only chooses one major, but the above aspects of applying AP credit and taking summer courses still apply. If you are planning to attend a graduate program, investigate some undergrad programs that allow the undergrad degree to be completed with the graduate degree in a shorter amount of time. There are three and three programs with undergrad and law school, and there are also two and four programs with medical school.

People hear that I graduated college at the age of nineteen, and they think that I passed through it so quickly because I must have skipped grades in high school as a result of being smart. Rather, I just do not like to waste time and was able to leverage all the above opportunities in order to move through the university as quickly as possible. It is possible for you to do the exact same thing in almost any major you choose. Use AP and IB credits from high school. Use dual enrollment credit and take summer courses. Do not take nonsensical courses like University 101. Streamline the process. Take personal responsibility for your future, so you can make it out with your time, money, and dignity.

Chapter XVII

Coronavirus Case Study

"The internet is becoming the town square for the global village of tomorrow."—Bill Gates

Tragically, in the beginning of 2020, the entire world was struck with a pandemic caused by the highly contagious virus known as COVID-19. Starting in Wuhan, China, the virus spread around the world, causing major social, economic, and political changes. These changes will have extremely far reaching effects, and it seems at the time of writing this that our society and this generation will forever be scarred with memory of this appalling nightmare. Besides the collapse of the stock market, millions of jobs lost, and hundreds of thousands of deaths from the virus, there was another fundamental change to the American society. The higher education system in the United States, in seconds, switched from in-person instruction to online instruction.

During spring break, when looking at my email and listening to the roaring waves on the beach in South Carolina, I saw that the university was postponing classes for a week on top of the break. Many of the students were happy about not having to attend classes for another week, but I was thoroughly disappointed in that I wanted to attend classes and actually learn things. The overwhelming amount of joy I saw from canceled classes spoke to the problem of academic apathy I saw every day on campus. Later, during the week, the university would move all classes to an online setting for the rest of the semester. It felt like I was at last seeing the final nail in the modern university. This will be the fundamental shift in how universities operate. The movement to online classes made me happy to an extent because I was arguing for this during my entire time at university that most of these things could be moved online for a lower price. But the universities are keeping tuition the same during this time, like they do with other online courses, making people question the real point of university. Therefore, I say, this period will be the watershed moment when the university system collapses. Students are already starting to ask why they are paying for an online class that is so expensive. What are these students paying for when there is just as good information online from other free sources?

Throughout this book, I have discussed how the university, in a fundamental sense, is moving from the classical university of higher education to the internet, where the access to information is almost completely free. Universities are already feeling the effects with declining student enrollment for the upcoming year. This is the biggest victory for my argument that many of these classes can be moved online. Consequently, universities will begin to hear calls for lower tuition rates because of this type of low-overhead education through the internet.

Universities around the country are beginning to see the effects of declining student populations as the cash provided by student loans dry up. Crazily, some universities and colleges are already closing shop because of the lack of enrollment and small endowments.[90]

Like I claimed before, endowments are important, especially in times like these. However, the endowments should not be larger than the GDP of other nations. Small liberal arts colleges with small endowments are going to be the first to be destroyed by the virus. This is despite the 14 billion the government has currently provided through the CARES Act, which is giving funds to struggling higher education institutions during this uncertain time.[91] However, the CARES Act can only do so much when a substantial number of students just simply decide not to attend the university.[92] It will be a difficult time for the universities with small endowments, but is this a bad thing? There are some major benefits to this breakdown of the smaller universities in that it will cause a larger push for lower tuition and cutting of overhead within universities to stay alive. This moment in history might be the changing factor that allows for greater tuition reductions and entirely new ways of education for the university system.

The universities have done a surprisingly good job in moving the classrooms to an online format using companies like Zoom, who make video-conferences possible. Moreover, sites already used by universities, like Blackboard, have video-conference possibilities that are becoming useful in this era. These technologies should continue to be used as they allow for greater flexibility in education, and they offer education on a year-round basis to allow all students to graduate quicker. The social aspects of having college online might be an adjustment for current university students, but the switch can easily be done as students have seen in the past couple of months. Many of the failures of higher education might slowly disappear if the university education, outside of STEM and graduate education, is moved online.

Students, especially incoming freshmen, will have to make a difficult decision over the coming years as to whether to attend university during the pandemic. This time is vitally important for the higher education system, possibly a make-or-break moment. Never have students wielded so much power because of their unified decisions to not attend or delay attendance. Students will have the ability to bring the universities, especially those small liberal arts colleges, to bankruptcy.[93] This period of time needs to be the catalyst for change in higher education, one that transforms it to an online system, even if professors are referring to the move in such a quick turnaround as traumatic. More than three quarters of American households have access to an internet connection and some form of computer or smartphone according to 2015 surveys.[94] That figure has increased in 2020 to include almost every American having access in some form to the internet. Therefore, the excuse for some colleges that their students simply lack internet access is somewhat unbelievable, especially when students are paying tens of thousands of dollars for a degree. The idea that they do not have access to the internet with a laptop or computer seems unlikely; therefore, the mass switch to using online classes should be relatively frictionless. The only difficulty would be STEM and some graduate courses that have labs and other hands-on activities vital to the learning process.

Universities began to hear pushes for classes to be graded as pass/fail, where they would not be factored into the GPA. Universities bowed to these demands and usually offered the pass/fail for students on a class-by-class basis, making it optional to choose which classes to make pass/fail.

Coronavirus Case Study

Some universities made all classes pass/fail for everyone in the spring semester regardless of the student's preferences. Some students were even calling for everyone to be passed regardless of their grades, a push for letter grades to be abolished outright.[95] This is a prime example of the low academic standards that characterize universities in that the pass/fail creates little incentive for the students to do as best they can. Rather, this would incentivize students to do just what is required to pass. This would be even more of a drop in academic standards that would make the degree useless in post-graduation employment. Many students are already apathetic about the education they are getting from the university, so a system of making everything pass/fail would decrease the amount of actual work they would have to do and would be very appealing to already disinterested students.

An important aspect of the pandemic is that it has created a dilemma for international students whose families are cash strapped already and facing the idea of not being able to pay tuition. The visas of international students do not allow them to work off campus, so it will be difficult for them to continue in their studies without any form of income. A major part of higher education's cash flow is from international students who pay usually more than the average American student. This is going to make the higher education system starve for more funds as their endowments dry up, combined with lower matriculation of both domestic and international students.[96] It will be difficult for these students to return to the United States to finish their education, and the post-pandemic world might be forever changed. These students are constantly in a fluctuating environment that is very stressful, and even these students are now questioning why they would want to graduate from these universities. They are seeing that it is difficult to shine in the United States by just gaining a university degree, so they question higher education when they see the cost and lack of benefit.

International students make up about 20 percent of the student body within the United States, and the number has dramatically increased since the early 2000s. The highest percentages of students enrolled in American universities come from China and India. The number is starting to decline because of the current administration's restrictions, but the university system is estimated to lose up to 25 percent of the international student body because of the pandemic.[97] One example of how the international student body on campuses will affect the higher education system is at the University of Arizona, which is projecting that it will lose 80 percent of new international students and 30 percent of continuing international students with $33 million in lost revenue. Even though this is a worst-case scenario, where the university would lose a significant portion of their international student body, a recent survey discovered that 88 percent of colleges expect a decrease of international student enrollments. The outlook for international students already in the United States seems better, but the higher education system will begin to bleed, becoming cash-strapped.[98] Along with the decrease in enrollment of international students, the current ones have begun to ask the same question that many American students are already asking. Is this degree worth the price? If the education is online, why can't the international students simply take the course from another country via the internet? And, if this education is online alongside the same information for free via the internet, why are these colleges charging so much? This will be the rationale of students down the line when the higher education system moves to an online setting during the pandemic, and they will increasingly question the value of the degree they are pursuing. Hopefully, these courses will stay online in the future, leading to a decrease in the cost of tuition and streamlining of higher education. Ultimately, the future seems uncertain in almost every regard with the virus continuing to spread and social unrest within the political discourse. Anything can happen, but this moment will be the watershed for future change in higher education.

Part Four

Rectifying the Deficiencies

Chapter XVIII

Solving the Failures, Summarized

"I doubt if there is any problem in the world today—social, political or economic—that would not find a happy solution if approached in the spirit of the sermon on the mount."
—*Harry S. Truman*

There is a simple solution in response to the failures of the higher education system, which is to not attend universities. However, we should not throw the baby out with the bath water even though the baby—i.e. the important and good aspects of the university—is slowly disappearing. The universities have many options on what to do with these two years of education forced on students that might not even relate to their major. One of the things they can do is to simply abolish the system of having general education requirements outright or at least make them optional for students. Make these requirements optional. The idea is that students should not be taking courses that have no relation to their interest or career field if they do not want to. Making these requirements optional will give students more choice, and it might increase the overall student participation in these classes because the only students taking these classes would be ones who have the desire.

Most of these failures within the higher education system are interrelated. The solution to one problem would create a solution to another problem. For example, lowering student apathy could be a result of making the gen-eds an option because the students in their courses want to be there instead of being obligated. Further, another solution to the problem of student apathy could be increasing academic standards. Students will have to try harder and study more in order to maintain the grades they were getting before when academic standards were low. The solution to low academic standards is that professors need to get a focus on teaching as opposed to research, and they need to raise the bar of student participation, readings, and assessments. Also, if the academic standards were raised significantly, the individuals who were just coasting by without any real effort in the classes would drop out, making the degree worth even more as the accreditation becomes rarer.

A major solution to many of the social problems of the higher education system, like drinking, partying, illegal conduct, promiscuity, and hooking up would be personal responsibility. College students need to fundamentally adopt adulthood, but they are not doing so in the modern system of higher education. I am reminded of the Peter Pan story. The main character is a child who will never grow up. Captain Hook, the main antagonist in the story, is really the only adult character in the story. It is not very appealing for a child to grow up into an adult like Captain Hook. What child would want to be a tyrant and have a hook for an arm? Also, there is a crocodile chasing Captain Hook with a clock in its stomach. It is an archetypal story where the crocodile is the life clock, which haunts all adults and eventually devours them. Reciprocally, Captain Hook has no other choice other than to be a tyrant because he is so terrified of the time that he is losing to eventually be eaten by the crocodile. Peter Pan does not want to give up his childhood for such a horrible adulthood, becoming king of the lost boys in Neverland. Further, he gives up a real relationship with Wendy, who has accepted her mortality and wants to have a life, but Peter Pan must satisfy himself with Tinkerbell. Growing up is a sacrifice. One must leave behind the potential of childhood to replace that with the accomplishments of adulthood.[99]

College students have a dilemma. They can either choose to take on personal responsibility and move forward into maturity or let it come upon them unaware later in life. The effect of not maturing is not immediate, but it grows over time. It hits you with the force of nuclear bombs. The problem is that people, namely employers, will allow for a lack of requisite experience at a certain age. If you are 20, people really do not care that you act like an idiot, partying and drinking into a stupor, because your age is an excuse. The problem of the nuclear bombs hitting you is when you are 30 with absolutely no experience for anything productive and the excuse of being young is now gone. If you have not traded the potential of youth for the productivity of adulthood early on in life, then there will be serious problems later on. Being an old child is grotesque, but that is what happens if you delay adulthood for the pleasure of Neverland. When you are nothing but potential, there is nothing that you are. Once you adopt a trade, skill, job, or passion with at least some responsibility, you become something rather than just pure potential. Once you become something, there are more possibilities in place to which you can continue forward far past adolescence.

College students need to realize that growing up is a necessity, one which will come whether you want it to or not. If you give up adolescence as a young person, then later in life you will be able to come back to those aspects of yourself and rediscover the younger person you left behind when adopting responsibility. Therefore, in the latter part of people's lives, you can have the best of both worlds, the potential of your youth and the accomplishments of adulthood. Never in life do you not have to make a sacrifice. You make them regardless of the path you choose. College students who are immature and moving passively through life are sacrificing the better accomplishments of their future selves. The university is facilitating this entire process of living in Neverland. The sacrifice is high in the form of indentured servitude through debt. A high school student can go to university to not be anything, especially during the first two years and not declaring a major, instead of going to college in order to be something. That is why I desire that the first two years of college were made optional because there are those who want to attend university to be something, a very particular something. These people do not want to prolong adolescence in the form of gen-ed classes.

The issue of postmodern indoctrination can be solved through active engagement in class discussion, where students begin to challenge the perceptions of the professor. The professors in many universities are viewed as demigods, who hold the keys to all information in the world, but they are just human like everyone else. They have their biases, particularly of a left-wing variety. Students need to confront the professor on the ideology of anti-Western sentiment and socialist viewpoints. These ideas are reprehensible, but even if you wholeheartedly believe in these ideas, it is still a great practice to spar with professors. Students need not worry about offending the professors in the pursuit of knowledge. This skill of discussing things in-depth will serve you for the rest of your life. Conservatives on campus need to not shy away from speaking in classes, and they need to confront the postmodern and neo-Marxist ideas of the professors, thereby giving other students another way to view things. Students will generally accept anything the professor says, so the conservative in the class needs to interrupt that indoctrination of the students to which they might view something in another way. Throughout my entire time in college, I have only seen one student try to challenge a professor, and it was regarding a neo-Marxist idea, where the professor was arguing the moral benefit of socialism. She was from Europe and churching up the idea of massive collective ownership of the means of production. One brave soul ventured to argue with her about the detrimental effects of socialism. More conservatives need to intellectually engage with professors in the pursuit of truth, for the sake of other students who accept the professor's ideology without thinking critically.

Many conservatives on college campuses around the country see the safe spaces as idiocy, university administrators attempting to protect the feelings of students while stifling freedom of expression. The university needs to stop coddling their students because they will not be prepared once they enter the harsh real world that lacks spaces to protect feelings. There is a movement that is calling these graduates "snowflakes" because they go into the real world to crumble because it is not a soft and cushy place like university. There needs to be more debate and more hurt feelings. There needs to be more people engaged in discussion because the chance that a real important discussion will not result in upset feelings is essentially zero. Safe spaces need to be abolished, and the university must maintain constant free speech regardless of how provocative it is to most students. The more provocative the better as it will allow students to think critically and articulate their positions better.

With regards to college admissions, the university should not determine their acceptances or rejections based on ethnicity or race. Nor should they determine their admissions process on the donations of families or legacies of past generations. These factors do not add anything to the university, which progresses the fundamental goal of higher education. Diversity of backgrounds is important, but diversity in the sense of race or ethnicity is not important. Universities must adopt a need-blind and race-blind approach to admissions. They need to look only at the credentials of the candidates who apply. There needs to also be a greater limit on how many colleges you can apply to through the Common Application because students, if they have the money, apply to 20 universities without batting an eye, and this causes the universities to speed through the admissions process, accepting and rejecting students after seconds of evaluation. Students are wasting their money by doing this because they can only attend one university. Also, because of all these applications, the universities must increase the size of their administration. The Common Application should limit students to three or five picks when it comes to universities. This will allow students to apply to a reach and safety school, but not every school they think looks interesting.

The university has the potential to become what it once was. The only way forward for the universities is to go back to what they once were: the foundation of human experience and wisdom, striving to advance the expanse of that wisdom. The university system will continue to deteriorate unless there is radical change in the overall system, especially in the cost of tuition. The administrators have conspired to take the future earnings of students through loans, and the solution to this is stop issuing loans to every high school student who wants to go to college. There needs to be a dramatic decrease in student loans offering. The government needs to realize that not every student needs to go to university and stop incentivizing attendance through loans guaranteed by the government. There could be a merit-based system where loans are only given to high achieving students, or there could be a process where loans are given only to those who know what their plan is in a particular field. Give loans to students who want to go into valuable fields that the economy and the nation require at that specific time like STEM fields. Stopping the massive supply of loans will put a halting pressure to the increasing debt load of student loans, hopefully getting it more under control. Making these loans competitive will make students who really want to go to college do even better than they were doing before. No lender in his or her right mind would give an 18-year-old thousands of dollars without some reasonable expectation of getting the money back, but the government does it all the time. The government needs to get out of this system or at least reduce its involvement by a significant degree. The argument for free university is not the solution because it would cost the taxpayer too much and it is morally unfair to those that actually paid off their loans. More and more people would then attend the university, exacerbating the problems of the university. We need a decrease in the supply of graduating students, not an increase. There are plenty of more valuable options outside of the university system anyways, so it is not a decrease in the opportunity to a better life because college does not guarantee a better life. The longer this system continues down this road, the younger people will be set up to fail.

Chapter XIX

Options Besides University

"The Chinese use two brush strokes to write the word 'crisis.'
One brush stroke stands for danger: the other for opportunity. In
a crisis, be aware of the danger--but recognize the opportunity."
—*John F. Kennedy*

If you want to avoid the significant problems associated with higher education and the risk of unavailable post-graduation employment opportunities, there are many options besides the traditional four-year university. Firstly, these options are not at a lower position in the economy or social structure than going to college. They might have certain stigmas associated with them, but many of these options are just as good as going to a university in the current conditions of the economy and might provide arguably more benefits than the traditional college education. By picking some of these options, individuals should not completely abandon higher education in the fundamental sense of the word. Everyone in society, no matter what occupation, should continue to gain education for the sake of becoming educated. The study of history, science, and current events are vital to the progression of society, and these come in handy when voting in a democracy. Education should always be held up as the ideal, but the university, where education is slowly eroding, should not be held to the same standard. For those who decide to not attend the traditional four-year university, they might be able to become smarter than a college graduate through simply being an auto-didactic through reading and learning on their own and without having to pay tens of thousands of dollars.

The first option for those not warning to attend university is the military, which will set you up with many benefits along with the moral reward of serving your country. In certain nations, like Israel, military service is required of all its citizens, and this system might have benefits in this country if a similar system was introduced. Increasingly, this is not an option for most Americans because they are not able to pass the physical training standards, as the country begins to become more and more overweight. If you are able to join the military, though, it is a great opportunity for not only an experience that will continue to help you outside the military, but it is a great career for the long run. Simply serving in the military for a period will allow you to gain experience that almost no one in the country can obtain. Through service to the country, you will be able to receive post-9/11 GI benefits that will most likely pay for a college education if you still want to attend after your service. The military is a wonderful option for those who do not want to attend college right out of high school.

Go your own way and become an entrepreneur. Many of the most successful individuals of the 20th and 21st century did not even earn a college diploma, like Bill Gates, Steve Jobs, Michael Dell, and Mark Zuckerberg. More than 22 million people in the United States are self-employed without any other employees other than themselves.[100] There are several scholarships awarded to seniors in high school that demonstrate the skills to have independent employment, like National Associate for the Self-Employed. Moreover, the National Federation of Independent Business sponsors a fund that assists students who want to become an entrepreneur through places like trade schools or community colleges.[101] Most of the self-employed individuals are working from home, and the barrier to entry for becoming self-employed is low, assuming one has an internet connection. The internet provides a wealth of wisdom for starting a business, so it might be easier than you think, and the experience from running your own business might be better than sitting in a classroom and learning things for tens of thousands of dollars that are free online. As employers move away from universities there are things like the Thiel Foundation, where a scholarship provides a college student with funds if they drop out to start a company.[102] These programs need to be encouraged because the university system is only marginally adding to the innovation of the economy, and it is usually just producing individuals to be indentured servants at a time when they should be taking economic risks, like starting a business.

Another great option besides the traditional four-year program is going to community college where an associate degree is required for a career. Compared to the traditional university, community colleges offer an extremely low-cost alternative. If you still want to attend the four-year university, you can follow the community college education, saving some money in the process. This idea assumes it will take four years total to gain a degree, but as I have shown, it does not always take that much time. So, community colleges are better used as a degree that is required for a career, and these careers sometimes even pay more than the usual college student job after graduation. Careers as an MRI technologist (avg. salary $65k), nuclear technician (avg. salary $69k), and air traffic controller (avg. salary $122k) are lucrative and do not require a traditional bachelor's degree. One of the issues I have with community college, but one that is usually a positive for most people, is that you are usually near your hometown. This is not necessarily a bad thing, but the tone is that you take on responsibility at a slower pace. This is ill-advised in my opinion, and people during this period in life need to take on as much personal responsibility as they can handle for the sake of themselves, the community, and the country.[103]

As discussed before, there is a major skills gap within the United States economy with millions of jobs going unfilled because they are not "good" jobs in people's minds. During the height of the economic recession of 2008, more than 3 million jobs were just waiting to be filled, but there was a lack of skill within the workforce to fill these. Instead, more people went to college during this time to supposedly advance their career. This point lays out the stereotype of college degrees making people successful a priori. But that is not the truth. There are millions of people who work skilled-labor positions that make a decent living with the average trade skills position at $42,000 annually. That is only $3,000 less than the average salary of the college graduate, and the skills person is moving into the workforce usually two to four years sooner and without student loan debt. Positions in electrical, landscaping, construction, welding, painting, metal work, locksmithing, and photography are all good jobs that do not require a college education that puts you in massive amounts of debt.

Technical colleges provide the opportunity to learn the skills for these jobs, and students do not have to take classes that are not related to that person's career focus. There are also options for apprenticeships or fellowships that give you the ability to learn skills or entrepreneur abilities.[104]

A very lucrative option that provides the possibility for a high income outside of the traditional four-year degree is selling real estate. The barrier to entry in this profession is relatively low. You will have to take a few courses, usually online, and then take a state-licensing test. The expected growth of the housing market makes it lucrative, and the job growth in this sector is expected to be around 11 percent for the next decade. This might change as a result of certain economic conditions, but overall, it is a good opportunity for those who do not want to pursue the traditional four-year degree.

One of the things that boggled my mind during my university experience were those who were theater, art, and music majors, paying thousands and thousands of dollars for this type of education. These individuals should have considered not attending a four-year university because the skills they learn can be achieved without college. If you are a good artist or musician, the economy will reward those skills. The university education will not factor into it because even if you went to the best university in the world but were still terrible at painting or singing, then your art will not be worth anything. Building a following and clientele will be just like a business, and it would be better to use the money of a college education to move to an art-friendly city where it will be easier to demonstrate your talent. Colleges might provide education in the fields of art, music, or theater but are they necessary when that information and teaching can be done outside the university system for much less and when those careers do not require any accreditation to be successful.

Another option for those not wanting to pursue overpriced education in the four-year university is just getting any job in the local area that fits the skills that you have so far developed. There are several jobs that do not even require any formal education beyond high school, like a gaming/casino manager (avg. salary $65k), power plant operator (avg. salary $66k), detective/criminal investigator (avg. salary $74k), and elevator installer/repairer (avg. salary $77k). If after working a job after high school you then decide college is for you, then that is the time in which you should attend. There are several benefits to this option. Namely, you will be much more mature than the rest of your peers if you do indeed decide to attend university, which is a major plus when most students shirk responsibility during this period of life. Also, having a job during this time will give you more money to pay off the tuition. Taking a gap year like this will give you more time to evaluate your skill set and decide if college is the right choice instead of being pressured by social stigmas to simply just attend right after high school.

The major concern people have when considering their future is how they will put food on their table. The economy is one of the biggest issues for American voters, especially jobs. So, people are justly upset when they do not have secure employment. It is increasingly becoming the case where college students graduate and are either underemployed or jobless.[105] It is vital that people know which sectors of the economy need employment instead of just following the pack. They need to start following opportunities instead of simply going to college because that is the expected thing to do. And we need to encourage more people going into fields that are underrepresented but still provide a stable and reasonable source of income. This does not mean we need to get rid of higher education entirely, but certain people do not need to attend colleges and universities when their skills are better suited for other careers. These people would actually do better economically by not attending college and universities.

I do not want to persuade readers whether to attend university or not. It is ultimately based on the particular circumstances of the individual. But for those who do not want to attend, I want them to know that other options besides the traditional four years university exist and provide the same economic outcomes. There are always sacrifices that people have to make in making any decision, but I hope that the above options will give you some insight into how the outcomes of some non-college graduates compare with those that do attend. Fundamentally, we need to stop thinking that most people who attend a university are successful. We need to admire occupations that are vital to the economy, especially the ones considered dirty jobs. Ultimately, the circumstances will be different for every person, but the above options could be beneficial to those with the specific skills suited for the other options. Higher education has some value in the long run for certain people, but the decision to attend is bigger than high school graduates realize, so it is vital that these young people weigh all the options in front of them.

Chapter XX

The Good Out of the Bad and Ugly

"You see, in this world there's two kinds of people, my friend: those with loaded guns and those who dig."—Clint Eastwood in The Good, The Bad, and The Ugly

From the overall theme of this book, one might get the idea that there is nothing good about the higher education system in the United States, or that I think there is nothing to gain from the experience. There are several good things about university, but only for those for whom it is the right choice. Like I have discussed in the cost-benefit analysis chapter, not everyone should go to college. But, if it is the right decision for you to attend university, there are many positive aspects about the process despite all the issues laid out in this book. It is easy to be on the sidelines of a complicated situation and point out the flaws in the system to help bring it back on track. But there are several positive aspects of the system that I experienced during my time at the university even though they usually did not outweigh the failures of higher education. Furthermore, these aspects were usually not with the university themselves, but were with tangential components of higher education I enjoyed.

INTRO TO FAILURE

One of the enjoyable aspects was the people that I met, many of whom are my closest friends. I would not pay tens of thousands of dollars for the opportunity to make friends, but it was an enjoyable part of attending university. I hear the idea of making connections through university, but you can make just as many connections outside of the system too. Connections are important, but would you pay ten or even hundreds of thousands of dollars for them when networking fairs and other job opportunities lead to the same end. Regardless, friendships in college were an aspect I enjoyed during my experience.

Professors were another great aspect of the college experience. Some of them were good at discussing issues and talking about the topics of the class. For example, one of my summer classes was in Middle Eastern politics, and the professors were engaging in the material. He asked us questions on the issues and debated us on ideas. And, this intellectual sparring with the professor, something I found difficult with other students because of safe space ideology, was enjoyable. Further, these professors would give me recommendations for graduate school and help in other ways like enlightening me on opportunities around the school. This will be one of the major sticking points in the future for colleges as they will advocate that universities are still viable because they offer students the service of professorial guidance in your studies. However, this bedrock is eroding in higher education because I got the same experience with my professors in an online setting during COVID-19. The problem for the university is that professors or teachers can do the same thing online, again, for less money. So, eventually this sticking point will leave the halls of higher learning.

The Good Out of the Bad and Ugly

Professors have office hours and similar setups to offer students who utilize these features to further their studies, but I never used them and still maintained high grades. Moreover, I would be more inclined to use them if they were online through a video chat as it is usually nerve racking for students to go to office hours, so they usually do not attend.

ROTC was another enjoyable aspect of the university, one outside the higher education system. Even though I was not on a scholarship or contact, I was able to participate in the program as I was in the running for a scholarship because of my ability to succeed in the program. This goes more to my temperament and specific affection for the military lifestyle instilled into me through my father over the course of my entire childhood. But I think that these programs need to be expanded for the sake of solving some of the problems listed throughout the book. There is no illegal drug use because there are drug tests. The overall atmosphere is one of health where people actively exercise. There is an aroma of free speech as there are no postmodern professors or "snowflakes" trying to silence opposing opinions. Furthermore, the cost to benefit of these programs is extremely positive, and they give students a pathway for future employment. Even though there was still the main college problem of drinking alcohol within groups in ROTC, there was a higher degree of discipline and lower academic apathy among those in the program. I was unable to continue after my first year because I prioritized the idea of graduating early more than ROTC, but it was nonetheless one of the most enjoyable aspects of my two years in university. Because it was enjoyable, I will most likely continue with the Army following law school in the JAG.

INTRO TO FAILURE

Within higher education, traditional students come into a world where adolescence is propagated, and responsibility is abrogated while you are taking classes. This lack of responsibility was engraved in the mentality when I came to college, and many students took no responsibility besides sliding by in classes, speaking to the low academic standards and student apathy. I enjoyed this lack of responsibility for about the first month. But it very quickly became sour as I realized life has no purpose without responsibility, and the community needs, requires even, greater personal responsibility of people. So, it was entertaining for a time to have less responsibility, but that pleasure quickly disappeared as I realized the realities of adulthood and life in general. For some students, the lack of responsibility that university often provides is a positive. But, overall it is a negative as you just delay the inevitable suffering of life that awaits when you must bear your individual cross after graduation and move forward through life taking obligation to your duties as a citizen of the country and the world.

Many people claim that a positive of college is that people can experience new things and learn different subjects. This is very true, and people sometimes do that even if it is to their future financial detriment. This would be the main selling point of university is that you can gain the college experience of learning a breadth of knowledge that the average person does not get to know. But, in the modern era of technology, access to information is not as difficult. The main selling point of learning new things can be done for free online. Proponents would argue that the experience of studying abroad is one of the biggest positives in that students can try new things. I completely agree that traveling is a major positive for the development of a person, but that does not need to be done within the college environment. If you really want to travel, you can go outside of the university where you are paying tens of thousands of dollars for such an experience.

Certain classes that actually provide a major benefit of being in the classroom should be saved from the movement into online courses, and these particular classes are a positive aspect of higher education. These courses are generally the skills courses that confer a benefit with the degree despite it still being overpriced. Usually, these classes are in the fields of STEM where the applicable knowledge is learned through labs and hands-on experience. Graduate schools, where in-person instruction is important, like in medical and law school, should also maintain in-person education because it is fundamental to the education itself. However, many of the college courses in the current higher education system can be easily moved online while with others it would be nearly impossible.

Personally, I enjoyed many parts of my time in college even though I did not engage with the common idea of what people call the "college experience." Most of the things I enjoyed were tangentially related to higher education, like the library, gym, and campus itself. When I realized that the education I was receiving could be gained from other sources, I asked what was I paying for? This idea struck me whenever I would watch YouTube videos that discussed the same information we were learning in class in the same level of detail. Even though it was not a professor speaking in the video, I realized it did not need to be a professor because facts are facts. Professors do not have supreme authority on information; they do not have the right to be the sole arbiters of education. Documentaries and books provided just as good information as my professors. So, when I have discussed the point of university with my friends, they argue that it is about the college experience and the accreditation. I understand the idea of accreditation, but what do people mean by this subjective idea of "college experience?"

I repeatedly heard this one phrase of the "college experience" that was meant to characterize the higher education system. Most students would lament that this idea was the best aspect of higher education. When I wanted to graduate early, many of my friends said I would miss out on this concept. But, what did they mean when they used these words? They would argue that it is the freedom to make mistakes, learn, and party. Many people claimed it was the lack of rules they gained from not being under their parents' supervision. More people argued that it was a place to learn something about yourself or gain information that cannot be gained elsewhere. I would then ask my friends whether they could gain such information outside of the university system or would graduating early necessarily impede any of the positive aspects for my future career. They usually would not have answers for these two questions as they never thought that the learning about yourself that accompanies the college experience could be done elsewhere. They thought that graduating early would impede many of the positives of the university system. However, many of the aspects of the college experience can be done elsewhere, and an early graduation will not significantly impede the experience that people gain from being in college if it will at all.

Usually, when students talk about the "college

experience," they are not talking about the education they are getting in class because they know that most of that information can be gained via the internet for free. The idea of the "college experience" for most students is the idea of finding yourself or partying. These two should not be the point of higher education in the first place. Additionally, finding yourself is not exclusive to the university and can be done outside of it. Also, you are not going to find yourself because college does not have the harsh challenges of the real world. Through low academic standards and the de facto lack of possible failure means that college is the last place a person should look if the goal is to develop into an adult. Many of the challenges faced by college students do not even remotely compare to the difficulties they will face in the real world. College students are kidding themselves if they are taking out loans for college with the belief that they are growing or finding themselves. More commonly, people refer to the "college experience" as partying and having fun with your friends. The reason that partying is so common on college campuses is that most college students are relatively young, and this is the age when most students make poor decisions, especially regarding drinking alcohol.

Overall, the term does not have one meaning, but when most people refer to the college experience, they usually include parties, connections, clubs, and education with a special emphasis on aspects other than learning. The university should not have its focus on things like partying and under-age drinking. Students should also realize that the cost of university does not necessarily create the benefit of the college experience, and it is possible to gain such an experience outside of the university. Therefore, incoming students to the universities need to take a hard look at what their motivations are when deciding to attend the university and risking your financial future as a result.

Chapter XXI

Shifting Economic and Social Systems

"Everyone thinks of changing the world, but no one thinks of changing himself."—Leo Tolstoy

I would ask fellow classmates why they are attending university and what they are getting out of the process. What was their end game? Inevitably, this line of questioning would lead to their admission that it was for employment following graduation. But it took a lot of questioning to reach this simple conclusion because so many would claim they are in college for connections or making memories. This was a clue to me that many of my fellow college students had never done any retrospection on their own purpose for being at university. For all students, the university is a means to an end. It is a stepping stool to the career that students want to focus on in life. The major they choose will hopefully lead to employment following graduation. Therefore, in such a shifting economic landscape, why are students attending university with the subconscious aim of getting employment following graduation even though there is not even the slightest guarantee of secure employment post-graduation. With only about half of graduates getting the jobs they want; it is easy to wonder why so many high school graduates attend these universities in lieu of more opportunities in the job market outside of college.

A lot of this deals with the social stigma regarding attendance in that students, parents, and teachers believe that success is unlikely without a college diploma. Consequently, this makes high school students believe that their only option is university.

Everyone from parents and advisors to politicians and the governments are pressuring high school students to get a college degree, so a vast majority of high school students attend university. The government hands out loans to the students that are not absolvable in bankruptcy with the money going to a university that keeps raising tuition, meaning they can get away with spending whatever they want. The government makes money, usually in the graduate loan programs, on the interest accrued through these loans. It is a triangle of reciprocal relationships and similar to the military industrial complex. It is a sort of higher education indentured servitude complex composed of the students, universities, and the government. It ends with the theft of the future earning of students and the degradation of greater society. It is an abhorrent trend that needs to be reversed.

Students in high school need to have all their options laid out in front of them in order to make the most rational decision regarding their skills, interests, and abilities. Parents need to give these options to their children and together come to a decision that is reasonable rather than just assuming that university is the proper and best decision. High schools need to not assume that all their students would want or need to attend university, so it is vital for high schools to provide opportunities for students to gain apprenticeship or internships during the summer. For those who have already decided they would want to attend college, high schools need to utilize the summers for the students' benefit and take on the role of the university during the usual first two years. High schools should offer classes that would count toward college credit of gen-ed requirements. Summer break should overall be abolished as it is a relic of the past when growing and harvesting seasons were important to the student body. Overall, these seasonal patterns need not continue to be applied in the modern era, and that time can be used by the high school system to further education and develop their students.

Some students get into a sunk-cost fallacy when they attend university and realize it is not for them. They already spent so much time trying to do well, even though it's not the right thing for them, so they will continue on the path because they already put so much time into it and do not want to have what they have done a waste of time. University students who go to college and decide that it is not for them need to cut their losses quickly or else be doomed to continual pain in an area where their skills will not be applied to something they would have been good at outside the university. Even though the stigma of being a college dropout is becoming more acceptable because of entrepreneurs leaving school to make millions, the pressure of being a dropout makes it difficult for people to reasonably access their skills to determine if college is still the right choice. They have pressures on them from the university itself, their parents, and friends. College students might stay the course even though it is wrong for them just because they will be viewed as a failure if they drop out. I am not encouraging people to drop out of the university system, but I am encouraging students, who are struggling with the process, to reassess their skills. Take a real and long look at yourself to determine whether your skills would be better applied in another field outside of the university system. Do not focus on the cost of dropping out. Instead, look at the cost of not doing anything about your situation. Look at the cost going through life like a paper bag in the wind. Make the decision of dropping out rationally based on your individual skill level and without the pressure of others.

There is an inverse relationship in education where the productivity of education is declining while the costs are rising. There have been major stagnations in the high school system since the 1970s, regardless of racial or ethnic differences. The administrations of education in the United States is increasing without a subsequent rise in the quality of teaching. Also, the salaries of teachers are low, making teaching a non-attractive occupation. It is disappointing that teachers receive such poor salaries with such a profound job of importance to greater society. This problem will continue to affect the macroeconomic trends of the country, disproportionately affecting the poor who do not have the resources for adequate teaching in the household. Teachers are stifled with bureaucratic processes like mandatory administrative exams.[106] The federal government has poured billions into education with very little to show for it. This is the result of an overarching bureaucracy in the federal government that believes it can solve all problems in human life. The Department of Education has been around since 1979, but since its inception, there has been little to no increase in the productivity of the education system producing smarter children for this country. This unconstitutional organization that oversees education, a power that should be governed by the states, absolutely destroyed the freedom of students and school choice. The most notable program that was an absolute failure of the Department of Education was the Common Core, where schools were forced to undergo several incentives, penalties, and tests. This created confusion and bureaucratic red tape that imposed horrible education standards that were inaccurate and misguided. The federal government has played out many of these top-down approaches to education that have not improved the education of the youth in this nation. Moreover, the Department of Education is beginning to track the lives of students in the education system, making parents uneasy about their children's privacy being violated by an overarching government bureaucracy. Besides test scores, the department wants to track and collect the data of many student interactions within the classroom, like facial expressions. It is something straight out of Orwell's *1984*, and the process has not created any gains in education, even by the department's own admission.[107]

Overarching bureaucracy is usually a bad thing when it comes to government intervention, and the Department of Education is not helping the education system within the United States. The powers that the federal government has over education need to be given back to the states where the federal government can instead simply give grants to the states for funding of education. The primary education of the country has a direct relationship to the problem faced in the higher education system. If the primary education system were to improve, with states taking on the role of the

Department of Education, then there might be a subsequent improvement in the higher education system. What is happening with the government increasing bureaucracy in overseeing the education of the country is happening within the higher education system itself. The bureaucracy within the university, namely the senior administration and university presidents, are overreaching their boundaries but not adding anything to the quality of the education. They are blowing up the price of tuition while not increasing the value of the degree or the teaching. This one of the systems in higher education that needs to be destroyed because of the lack of benefit to the student that is at odds with its major costs. A massive administration that tries to centrally plan for all aspects of student life will usually fail in its aims while increasing the price of its conduct, which is what happens in the federal government and the modern higher education system.

Moving away from the social stigma of university attendance will be a great step towards the betterment of the youth and will change how universities operate. The economic environment of the country is shifting, and technology and automation will make many jobs superfluous, many of which are from college and university. This pressure will make it more obvious that a college diploma is not necessarily a gateway to an upper middle-class lifestyle. The longer that jobs in the economy go unfilled as a result of a skills gap and the university does not provide economic incentive because of students graduating with debt and a lack of job security, the more it will make people realize that the university might not be the best choice for high school graduates.

Abrogation of Personal Responsibility

"Death is nothing, but to live defeated and inglorious is to die daily."—Napoleon Bonaparte

Life is difficult. This is one of the fundamentals of human existence that I have concluded in my short time on this earth. For the Buddhists, life consists of suffering, pain, and misery. For Hobbes, life is nasty, brutish, and short. For Christians, life is bearing the cross of sin and pain. This does not mean that life is devoid of meaning. Understanding these truths of life will allow someone to voluntarily accept his or her mortality. Indeed, that is a difficult thing to do. Life becomes less painful when there is a purpose you are following. It is extensively more difficult to go through life when there is no path to follow or purpose that gives it meaning. A dilemma with higher education is that it allows young people to go to college without any purpose other than attending and doing something. Undeclared majors and gen-ed requirements make students go through the process without any specific pathway, prolonging the time when young people must adopt purpose and voluntarily accept adulthood.

I have seen this happen in my personal experience

with many of my fellow students in the higher education system who do not have a pathway in life, so they distract themselves with the instant gratifications of the present instead of preparing for the future. They went to college under the assumption that they were going to figure it out when they got there. They took gen-eds and changed their majors many times. It is difficult to have a purpose that gives meaning to life without a set pathway to follow, and the universities are facilitating this nebulous environment devoid of meaning where students can take whatever classes, studying in what is essentially a "Neverland." Many people, including students, find meaning and purpose within the umbrella of religion, which maintains a pathway in life. The university system does not have a pathway for at least the first two years for most students, and when they find their purpose, they are loaded with enough debt to render them indentured servants for the next twenty years of their lives.

Without a pathway, life seems meaningless, but imagine if you wholeheartedly stuck to the pathway for a couple of years. If you were to reasonably assess your particular skills and made a game plan with a specific pathway to which you followed, you would be surprised to find that years later you would be in a better position than before. Lay bare all the excuses that might sway you off the path. Attending university with a pathway will lead to better conclusions than without one, where you are going through life haplessly.

Studies have demonstrated that this lack of purpose is increasingly affecting young men, especially those who are college-aged, non-Western minority men because they must figure it out for themselves. The argument is that men do not necessarily have those biological predispositions for meaning in life, like women with pregnancy. Women generally must figure out the important aspects of their lives sooner than men because of this biological predisposition. Nonetheless, college students, regardless of gender, have a difficult time in finding a purpose within higher education because of an environment where there is a lack of direction and a major lack of responsibility. If college students found a purpose, they would be less inclined to engage in instant gratification because there is a light at the end of the tunnel. When there is importance given to the future, the actions of the present become far more impactful. Higher education needs to change for the betterment of students, so these students can attend college to be something, and so they can have a pursuit right when they get there and not fall to the temptations of instant gratification. Students need to pick a pathway that justifies the difficulty of life. Universities need to facilitate this by solving the problems laid out in this book. Maybe, then, the university will be returned to its prestige. Maybe, it will be where people go with a purpose, where maturity is celebrated, and where academic standards are high. Maybe, it will become the place where technology is fully utilized, where the culture is established around scholastics instead of drinking or hooking up, and where people can go without becoming indentured servants. Maybe, they will return to a place where the fundamental idea of higher education, the collection of all human wisdom and the pursuit of its betterment, is fully realized.

Questioning a fundamental structure of society, the higher education system, is usually a hypocritical and trivial pursuit, as our own households are nowhere near squared away. But it is the proper purpose of all people to first place their own lives in order before trying to reorder a city or social system. For it is far more difficult to control yourself than an organization of complex interactions and, therefore, personal responsibility is paramount to university students. First, place yourself in impeccable order before you begin trying to tear down or reform the systems of the modern era. By no means is my life in perfect order, but I have learned from the hard-fought wisdom of those who have come before me. Criticizing this system, I am not resentful of universities, and I am proud of graduating from university. But everyone has a responsibility to speak the truth. It is fundamental to Western society that all people clearly articulate truth to bring forth a better understanding of humanity and its ills. As clearly as I could, with all my ignorance as it may be, and along my biased predispositions, I have stated what I think is the truth, trying to bring forth a better reality for those in society.

Writing this book, I felt that there were aspects with the higher education system that were centrally broken, and I would be complicit in the continued failure of the higher education system if I were to say nothing. I would be willfully blind to the failures of higher education, and I would be capitulating to the system which is continuing to set students up for failure. If something is not working to produce educated, employed, and honorable citizens of the nation, it is the people who graduate from such institutions to try with zeal to rectify those injustices. I do not know what the future holds for higher education, but I can reasonably suspect that it will not be the same as it is now in the next thirty to forty years. My advice to the youth of the nation is not that education is somehow not wise to attain, but the system itself has flaws that allow it to not be the right choice for everyone.

Abrogation of Personal Responsibility

Education is the cornerstone of human society. It teaches us what to do and what not to do. Everyone should aspire to be educated, but attendance within the higher education system does not guarantee a solid education today. I am not optimistic regarding the fate of the university system. This might be the era when universities begin to collapse. However, I am very optimistic about the youth of this nation making rational decisions about their future, and the fighting spirit of this generation to continue forward with purpose, dedication, innovation, and exuberance.

Acknowledgments

Throughout my life, I have been significantly blessed by those around me who have guided me through difficult times and have shaped me into the person I am today. I am eternally grateful for their leadership, intelligence, and direction. Supremely, my parents have developed me with important values and benevolent morals with an emphasis on discipline and education. They laid the foundation of who I am, and they created my understanding of society and the culture of which I am forever beholden. They have provided me with innumerable opportunities that allow me to continue my journey through life. They have always worked very hard to accomplish everything they have.

Thank you to my sister for fostering my competitive spirit and thick skin. She has always led the way for me and taught me the ropes in my life. She is the Plato to my Alexander the Great, teaching me many of the ways of the world.

Thank you to my friends for being there for me in difficult times and helping me reach my goals in life. I have always brought my ideas to my friends for discussion, so I was able to define my arguments concisely and understand the topics more. My freshman year roommate and great friend, Kyle Stegmann, has been the devil's advocate in the writing of this book, discussing my arguments and pointing out flaws. I am appreciative of his friendship and advice during this time

Acknowledgments

and other points in the past.

Thank you to my teachers in my life who have taken personal interest in my success. They have helped me along the way during my education, and I am very grateful for this. Especially during high school, my teachers were able to promote my intellectual curiosity and enable my pursuit of knowledge. I want to give a great appreciation to Dr. Jordan Peterson. His lectures and book *12 Rules for life: An Antidote to Chaos* has been a guiding light in my adoption of personal responsibility and movement upright through life. Many of the rules have brought me out of darkness, accepting the difficulty of life. His great wisdom is a dominant narrative throughout this book, and I am forever grateful for his teachings.

Thank you to my God, who has always been there with me through both easy and difficult times. To all the people who have guided me through life, thank you. Thank you to all the people who have helped this book become a possibility from start to finish.

INDEX

Index

painting, 161, 162

pajamas, 48

pandemic, 145, 148, 149, 150

partying, xiii, 58, 62, 71, 104, 111, 131, 137, 139, 151, 152, 172

pass/fail, 148

patriarchy, 87, 133

Peter Pan, 151

Pew Research Center, 75, 84

Ph.D., 84

philosophy, xv, 17

Plato, 186

plumbing, 28

polarized, 79

police battalions, 89

political science, xi, 34, 46, 86, 126, 129, 131

political science major, xi, 34, 129

politically correct, 12

pornography, 71

post-9/11 GI benefits, 159

postgraduate, 39

postmodernist, 12, 84, 90

pre-calculus, xi

prestigious, xii, 119, 121

printing press, 12

private universities, xi, 22, 113

professional school, 13, 112

professors, ix, 5, 41, 42, 43, 44, 45, 46, 50, 51, 60, 76, 81, 82, 83, 84, 86, 90, 131, 134, 143, 148, 151, 153, 167, 168, 171

professorships, 3

Protestant, 15

PSAT, 24, 120

public equities, 3

Public Service Loan Forgiveness Plan, 9

racist, 18, 90, 92, 93, 134, 135

Reagan, 102

real estate, 162

Reconstruction, 18

religious, 15, 16, 70

Renaissance man, 119

Republican, 84

Reserve Officer Training Corps, 56

Notes

1. Friedman, Z. (2020, February 05). Student Loan Debt Statistics In 2020: A Record $1.6 Trillion. Retrieved July 08, 2020, from https://www.forbes.com/sites/zackfriedman/2020/02/03/student-loan-debt-statistics/

2. Kleanthous, B. (2018, August 3). How Much Is a TRILLION? Retrieved July 08, 2020, from https://www.thecalculatorsite.com/articles/finance/how-much-is-a-trillion.php

3. Hess, A. J. (2020, June 12). How student debt became a $1.6 trillion crisis. Retrieved July 08, 2020, from https://www.cnbc.com/2020/06/12/how-student-debt-became-a-1point6-trillion-crisis.html

4. Hess, A. J. (2019, October 30). Harvard's endowment is worth $40 billion-here's how it's spent. Retrieved July 08, 2020, from https://www.cnbc.com/2019/10/28/harvards-endowment-is-worth-40-billionheres-how-its-spent.html

5. World Population Review. (2020). Retrieved July 08, 2020, from https://worldpopulationreview.com/countries/countries-by-gdp/

6. Burstein, E. M., & Caldera, C. G. (2020, March 19). COVID-19 Leaves Harvard in 'Grave' Financial Situation, Experts Say. Retrieved July 08, 2020, from https://www.thecrimson.com/article/2020/3/19/harvard-

coronavirus-endowment-impact/

7. Simon, C. (2017, September 05). Bureaucrats And Buildings: The Case For Why College Is So Expensive. Retrieved July 08, 2020, from https://www.forbes.com/sites/carolinesimon/2017/09/05/bureaucrats-and-buildings-the-case-for-why-college-is-so-expensive/

8. Milton Ezrati, Contributing Editor at The National Interest, A. (2018, July 31). Closing the Skills Gap. Retrieved July 08, 2020, from https://www.city-journal.org/html/closing-skills-gap-16083.html

9. Johnson, D. M. (2019, September 23). What Will It Take to Solve the Student Loan Crisis? Retrieved July 08, 2020, from https://hbr.org/2019/09/what-will-it-take-to-solve-the-student-loan-crisis

10. Burkhardt, J. (2017). Historical & Structural Roots: The American System of Higher Education - Bias of Consciousness. Retrieved July 03, 2020, from https://www.coursera.org/lecture/leading-for-equity-diversity-inclusion/historical-structural-roots-the-american-system-of-higher-education-8GCGl

11. COLLEGES IN THE COLONIAL TIMES.: News: The Harvard Crimson. (n.d.). Retrieved July 03, 2020, from https://www.thecrimson.com/article/1883/4/20/colleges-in-the-colonial-times-prof/

12. Ibid, p.34

13. Tucker, L. (1979). Centers of Sedition: Colonial Colleges and the American Revolution. *Proceedings of the*

Notes

Massachusetts Historical Society, 91, 16-34. Retrieved July 3, 2020, from www.jstor.org/stable/25080846

14. Leisch, J. (2018, October 23). Education during the 1860s. Retrieved July 03, 2020, from https://www.battlefields.org/learn/articles/education-during-1860

15. The History Engine. (n.d.). Southern Higher Education after the Civil War. Retrieved July 08, 2020, from https://historyengine.richmond.edu/episodes/view/2554

16. Stefon, M. (2019, October 01). Historically black colleges and universities. Retrieved July 08, 2020, from https://www.britannica.com/topic/historically-black-colleges-and-universities

17. Schrecker, E. (2009, June 16). The Bad Old Days: Higher Ed During the Great Depression. Retrieved July 08, 2020, from https://www.chronicle.com/article/The-Bad-Old-Days-Higher-Ed/44526

18. Crimson News Staff. (1956, December 7). College Life During World War II Based on Country's Military Needs: News: The Harvard Crimson. Retrieved July 08, 2020, from https://www.thecrimson.com/article/1956/12/7/college-life-during-world-war-ii/

19. Sarah Lawrence College. (n.d.). The College during World War II. Retrieved July 08, 2020, from https://www.sarahlawrence.edu/archives/digital-collections/wwii/background.html

20. Lazerson, Marvin. "The Disappointments of Success: Higher Education after World War II." The Annals of the

Notes

American Academy of Political and Social Science, vol. 559, 1998, pp. 64–76. JSTOR, www.jstor.org/stable/1049607. Accessed 22 June 2020.

21. Ap. (1984, September 02). COLLEGE ENROLLMENT LINKED TO VIETNAM WAR. Retrieved July 08, 2020, from https://www.nytimes.com/1984/09/02/us/college-enrollment-linked-to-vietnam-war.html

22. Duffin, P., & 13, M. (2020, March 13). U.S. college enrollment statistics 1965-2028. Retrieved July 08, 2020, from https://www.statista.com/statistics/183995/us-college-enrollment-and-projections-in-public-and-private-institutions/

23. How Many Universities & Colleges are in the US? (2019, August 05). Retrieved July 08, 2020, from https://www.educationunlimited.com/blog/how-many-universities-colleges-are-in-the-us/

24. McLaughlin, K. (2020, April 15). Dozens of colleges are dropping SAT and ACT requirements for 2021 applicants. Retrieved July 08, 2020, from https://www.insider.com/colleges-dropping-sat-act-requirements-2021-applicants-2020-4

25. Silvers, K. (2020, March 31). Why General Education Classes Are More Important Than You Think. Retrieved July 08, 2020, from https://www.herzing.edu/blog/why-general-education-classes-are-more-important-you-think

26. Ransby, A. (2019, February 13). 7 Universities Where You Can Take a Class on "Harry Potter". Retrieved July 08, 2020, from https://www.scholarshippoints.com/campuslife/7-

Notes

universities-where-you-can-take-a-class-on-harry-potter/

27. Cavalli, E. (2017, June 04). U.C. Berkeley Now Offers StarCraft Class. Retrieved July 08, 2020, from https://www.wired.com/2009/01/uc-berkeley-int/

28. Haverdink, M. (2019, October 15). My Thoughts On General Education Classes and Requirements. Retrieved July 08, 2020, from https://www.theodysseyonline.com/thoughts-general-education-classes-requirements

29. Jack, Z. M. (2018, April 5). Inside Higher Ed. Retrieved July 08, 2020, from https://www.insidehighered.com/views/2018/04/05/colleges-should-consider-halving-gen-ed-curriculum-requirements-opinion

30. Warner, J. (2018, July 15). Gen Ed Is a Problem of Pedagogy, Not Subject Matter: Inside Higher Ed. Retrieved July 08, 2020, from https://www.insidehighered.com/blogs/just-visiting/gen-ed-problem-pedagogy-not-subject-matter

31. Hoeft, M. E. (2012). Why University Students Don't Read: What Professors Can Do. Retrieved July 8, 2020, from https://digitalcommons.georgiasouthern.edu/cgi/viewcontent.cgi?article=1343&context=ij-sotl

32. R. Arum, J., & ET. Pascarella, P. (1970, January 01). Limited Learning on College Campuses. Retrieved July 08, 2020, from https://link.springer.com/article/10.1007/s12115-011-9417-8

Notes

33. Yglesias, M. (2012, May 23). College Students Don't Study Enough-but Not Because They're Lazy. Retrieved July 08, 2020, from https://slate.com/business/2012/05/college-students-don-t-study-enough-but-not-because-they-re-lazy.html

34. National Center for Education Statistics. (2019). College Student Employment. Retrieved July 8, 2020, from https://nces.ed.gov/programs/coe/pdf/coe_ssa.pdf

35. Isbell, L. (2017, March 14). Inside Higher Ed. Retrieved July 08, 2020, from https://www.insidehighered.com/advice/2017/03/14/professor-examines-why-her-students-seem-act-so-helpless-essay

36. GradeInflation.com. (2016, March 29). National Trends in Grade Inflation, American Colleges and Universities. Retrieved July 08, 2020, from http://www.gradeinflation.com/

37. Uloop. (2014, April 22). Cheating In College: Where It Happens, Why Students Do It and How to Stop It. Retrieved July 08, 2020, from https://www.huffpost.com/entry/cheating-in-college-where_b_4826136

38. National Institute on Alcohol Abuse and Alcoholism. (2019, December 24). Fall Semester-A Time for Parents To Discuss the Risks of College Drinking. Retrieved July 08, 2020, from https://www.niaaa.nih.gov/publications/brochures-and-fact-sheets/time-for-parents-discuss-risks-college-drinking

39. Voas, R. B., Johnson, M., Turrisi, R. J., Taylor, D.,

Notes

Honts, C. R., & Nelsen, L. (2008). Bringing alcohol on campus to raise money: impact on student drinking and drinking problems. Addiction (Abingdon, England), 103(6), 940–952. https://doi.org/10.1111/j.1360-0443.2008.02187.x

40. Editorial Staff. (2020, January 15). Concerns of Binge Drinking on College Campuses. Retrieved July 08, 2020, from https://www.alcohol.org/teens/college-campuses/

41. Ibid, Editorial Staff. (2020, January 15). Concerns of Binge Drinking on College Campuses.

42. Livescience.com. (2013, October 18). Fake-ID Use Is Common, Fuels Underage Drinking. Retrieved July 08, 2020, from https://www.livescience.com/40528-fake-ids-fuel-underage-drinking.html

43. Voas, R. B., Johnson, M., Turrisi, R. J., Taylor, D., Honts, C. R., & Nelsen, L. (2008). Bringing alcohol on campus to raise money: impact on student drinking and drinking problems. Addiction (Abingdon, England), 103(6), 940–952. https://doi.org/10.1111/j.1360-0443.2008.02187.x

44. Redlinger, S. (2018, September 06). Marijuana use among US college students remains at highest level in three decades. Retrieved July 08, 2020, from https://news.umich.edu/marijuana-use-among-us-college-students-remains-at-highest-level-in-three-decades/

45. Carter, S. (2019, September 06). Marijuana use among college students at highest level in 35 years. Retrieved July 08, 2020, from https://www.foxbusiness.com/features/marijuana-use-among-college-students-at-highest-level-in-35-years

Notes

46. Bauer-Wolf, J. (2019, September 9). Study: College students using marijuana, e-cigarettes at record rates. Retrieved July 08, 2020, from https://www.insidehighered.com/news/2019/09/09/study-college-students-using-marijuana-e-cigarettes-record-rates

47. DeGeurin, M. (2019, June 25). Cigarette smoking is at an all time low, but college students are increasingly turning to vaping, and schools are scrambling to regulate it. Retrieved July 08, 2020, from https://www.insider.com/college-students-are-increasingly-vaping-on-campus-2019-6

48. Ludden, D. (2018, August 28). Is Hook-Up Culture Dominating College Campuses? Retrieved July 08, 2020, from https://www.psychologytoday.com/us/blog/talking-apes/201808/is-hook-culture-dominating-college-campuses

49. Rice, B. (2019, February 13). Hookup culture on college campuses. Retrieved July 08, 2020, from https://www.newsrecord.org/college_life/hookup-culture-on-college-campuses/article_ef650db8-2f9d-11e9-89e0-77cc1675fd68.html

50. Klinger, L. (2016). Hookup Culture on College Campuses. Retrieved July 8, 2020, from https://scholarworks.gvsu.edu/cgi/viewcontent.cgi?article=1039&context=csal

51. Ibid, Klinger, L. (2016). Hookup Culture on College Campuses.

52. Ibid, Klinger, L. (2016). Hookup Culture on College Campuses.

Notes

53. Wade, L. (2017, August 25). The Rise of Hookup Sexual Culture on American College Campuses. Retrieved July 08, 2020, from https://scholars.org/brief/rise-hookup-sexual-culture-american-college-campuses

54. Campus Sexual Violence: Statistics. (n.d.). Retrieved July 08, 2020, from https://www.rainn.org/statistics/campus-sexual-violence

55. Jacobs, T. (2015, August 28). Pornography Consumption on the Rise. Retrieved July 08, 2020, from https://psmag.com/environment/surprise-we-all-love-porn

56. Brenner, G. (2018, March 05). 4 Ways Porn Use Causes Problems. Retrieved July 08, 2020, from https://www.psychologytoday.com/us/blog/experimentations/201803/4-ways-porn-use-causes-problems

57. Anderson, J. (2019, February 22). Conversations: Featuring Jordan Peterson... - YouTube. Retrieved July 8, 2020, from https://www.youtube.com/watch?v=kZBKmx52eas

58. Smith, A., & Anderson, M. (2020, May 30). Social Media Use 2018: Demographics and Statistics. Retrieved July 08, 2020, from https://www.pewresearch.org/internet/2018/03/01/social-media-use-in-2018/

59. Griffin, R. (2015, July 22). Social Media Is Changing How College Students Deal With Mental Health, For Better Or Worse. Retrieved July 08, 2020, from https://www.huffpost.com/entry/social-media-college-mental-health_n_55ae6649e4b08f57d5d28845

60. College students' mental health is a growing concern, survey finds. (2013, June). Retrieved July 08, 2020, from https://www.apa.org/monitor/2013/06/college-students

61. Joseph, S. (2019, August 29). Depression, anxiety rising among U.S. college students. Retrieved July 08, 2020, from https://www.reuters.com/article/us-health-mental-undergrads-idUSKCN1VJ25Z

62. Belk, N., Degolian, K., & Barham, K. (2019, April 8). Leading Causes of Death Among College Students. Retrieved July 08, 2020, from http://idst190.web.unc.edu/2019/04/college-student-death-causes/

63. Mammoser, G. (2018, December 10). Social Media Increases Depression and Loneliness. Retrieved July 08, 2020, from https://www.healthline.com/health-news/social-media-use-increases-depression-and-loneliness

64. Hong, S., & Kim, S. (2016). Political Polarization on Twitter: Social media May Contribute to Online Extremism. Retrieved July 08, 2020, from https://scholar.harvard.edu/sounman_hong/political-polarization-twitter-social-media-may-contribute-online-extremism

65. Leetaru, K. (2018, October 25). Social Media Companies Collect So Much Data Even They Can't Remember All The Ways They Surveil Us. Retrieved July 08, 2020, from https://www.forbes.com/sites/kalevleetaru/2018/10/25/social-media-companies-collect-so-much-data-even-they-cant-

remember-all-the-ways-they-surveil-us/

66. Peterson, J. (2018, June 11). Dangerous People Are Teaching Your Kids - YouTube. Retrieved July 8, 2020, from https://www.youtube.com/watch?v=LquIQisaZFU

67. Maitra, S. (2020, February 19). National Association of Scholars - The Economist Tries to Mislead about Liberal Bias in Academia by Sumantra Maitra. Retrieved July 08, 2020, from https://www.nas.org/blogs/article/the-economist-tries-to-mislead-about-liberal-bias-in-academia

68. Jaschik, S. (2017, February 27). Research confirms that professors lean left, but questions assumptions about what this means for conservatives. Retrieved July 08, 2020, from https://www.insidehighered.com/news/2017/02/27/research-confirms-professors-lean-left-questions-assumptions-about-what-means

69. Howard, B. (2017, September 21). Colleges Tackle Free Speech, Trigger Warnings, Safe Spaces. Retrieved July 08, 2020, from https://www.usnews.com/education/best-colleges/articles/2017-09-21/colleges-tackle-free-speech-trigger-warnings-safe-spaces

70. Sacks, D., & Thiel, P. (1996, September/October). The Case Against Affirmative Action. Retrieved July 08, 2020, from https://stanfordmag.org/contents/the-case-against-affirmative-action

71. Hartocollis, A. (2020, February 18). The Affirmative Action Battle at Harvard Is Not Over. Retrieved July 08, 2020, from https://www.nytimes.com/2020/02/18/us/affirmative-action-

harvard.html

72. Grutter v. Bollinger. (n.d.). Oyez. Retrieved July 8, 2020, from https://www.oyez.org/cases/2002/02-241

73. Gratz v. Bollinger. (n.d.). Oyez. Retrieved July 8, 2020, from https://www.oyez.org/cases/2002/02-516

74. Slattery, E. (2015, December 2). How Affirmative Action at Colleges Hurts Minority Students. Retrieved July 08, 2020, from https://www.heritage.org/courts/commentary/how-affirmative-action-colleges-hurts-minority-students

75. The New York Times. (2019, March 14). College Admissions Scandal: Your Questions Answered. Retrieved July 08, 2020, from https://www.nytimes.com/2019/03/14/us/college-admissions-scandal-questions.html

76. Jump, J. (2019, June 10). Inside Higher Ed. Retrieved July 08, 2020, from https://www.insidehighered.com/admissions/views/2019/06/10/when-donors-have-aspirations-admission-child-their-donations-may-not-be

77. Banks, R. R. (2019, November 12). Opinion: Donating money to help your child get into college isn't wrong. Retrieved July 08, 2020, from https://www.latimes.com/opinion/story/2019-11-12/college-admissions-donations-are-okay

78. U. (n.d.). Indentured Servants. Retrieved July 08, 2020, from https://www.ushistory.org/us/5b.asp

79. Whitmire, R. (2019, April 08). Alarming Statistics Tell

the Story Behind America's College Completion Crisis: Nearly a Third of All College Students Still Don't Have a Degree Six Years Later. Retrieved July 08, 2020, from https://www.the74million.org/article/alarming-statistics-tell-the-story-behind-americas-college-completion-crisis-nearly-a-third-of-all-college-student-still-dont-have-a-degree-six-years-later/

80. Backman, M. (2020, February 05). Student Loan Debt Statistics for 2019. Retrieved July 08, 2020, from https://www.fool.com/student-loans/student-loan-debt-statistics/

81. Education: The Rising Cost of Not Going to College. (2020, May 30). Retrieved July 08, 2020, from https://www.pewsocialtrends.org/2014/02/11/the-rising-cost-of-not-going-to-college/

82. Hess, A. J. (2019, June 19). College grads expect to pay off student debt in 6 years-this is how long it will actually take. Retrieved July 08, 2020, from https://www.cnbc.com/2019/05/23/cengage-how-long-it-takes-college-grads-to-pay-off-student-debt.html

83. Ccap. (2015, July 21). The Bennett Hypothesis Confirmed -- Again. Retrieved July 08, 2020, from https://www.forbes.com/sites/ccap/2015/07/21/the-bennett-hypothesis-confirmed-again/

84. Newton, D. (2018, June 27). Why College Tuition Is Actually Higher for Online Programs. Retrieved July 08, 2020, from https://www.forbes.com/sites/dereknewton/2018/06/25/why-

college-tuition-is-actually-higher-for-online-programs/
85. Rowe, M. (2016, June 6). Don't Follow Your Passion -
YouTube. Retrieved July 8, 2020, from
https://www.youtube.com/watch?v~CVEuPmVAb8o
86. Fioriello, D. (2018, October 10). The Importance Of A
High School Education. Retrieved July 08, 2020, from
https://drpfconsults.com/importance-high-school-education/
87. Can I Take an AP Test without Taking an AP Class?
(n.d.). Retrieved July 08, 2020, from
https://www.collegecountdown.com/test-prep/can-i-take-an-
ap-test-without-taking-an-ap-class.html
88. How Parent Involvement Leads to Student Success.
(2019, March 13). Retrieved July 08, 2020, from
https://www.waterford.org/education/how-parent-involvment-
leads-to-student-success/
89. Mulhere, K. (2015, February 25). Report marks growing
educational disadvantage for children of single-parent
families. Retrieved July 08, 2020, from
https://www.insidehighered.com/news/2015/02/25/report-
marks-growing-educational-disadvantage-children-single-
parent-families
90. Jdickler, J. (2020, June 10). Will pandemic force your
college to go bankrupt? Retrieved July 08, 2020, from
https://www.cnbc.com/2020/05/27/a-growing-number-of-
colleges-could-close-for-good-post-pandemic.html
91. CARES Act: Higher Education Emergency Relief Fund.
(2020, July 01). Retrieved July 08, 2020, from
https://www2.ed.gov/about/offices/list/ope/caresact.html

92. McLaughlin, K. (2020, April 26). The coronavirus could force smaller liberal arts and state colleges to close forever. Retrieved July 08, 2020, from https://www.insider.com/smaller-colleges-may-never-reopen-because-of-the-coronavirus-2020-4

93. Mitchell, N. (2020, May 07). Students to decide which institutions survive COVID-19. Retrieved July 08, 2020, from https://www.universityworldnews.com/post.php?story=20200507135847614

94. Lewis, J. M., & Ryan, C. (2017, September). Computer and Internet Use in the United States: 2015. Retrieved July 8, 2020, from https://www.census.gov/content/dam/Census/library/publications/2017/acs/acs-37.pdf

95. Hartocollis, A. (2020, March 28). With Coronavirus Disrupting College, Should Every Student Pass? Retrieved July 08, 2020, from https://www.nytimes.com/2020/03/28/us/coronavirus-college-pass-fail.html

96. Dickerson, C. (2020, April 25). 'My World Is Shattering': Foreign Students Stranded by Coronavirus. Retrieved July 08, 2020, from https://www.nytimes.com/2020/04/25/us/coronavirus-international-foreign-students-universities.html

97. Gordon, L. (2020, May 08). Fewer international students expected to return to colleges in California and nation, hurting finances. Retrieved July 08, 2020, from

https://edsource.org/2020/fewer-international-students-expected-to-return-to-colleges-in-california-and-nation-hurting-finances/631148

98. Redden, E. (2020, May 26). Colleges expect few new international students will make it to their campuses this fall. Retrieved July 08, 2020, from https://www.insidehighered.com/news/2020/05/26/colleges-expect-few-new-international-students-will-make-it-their-campuses-fall

99. Peterson, J. (2017, February 20). 2017 Maps of Meaning 06: Story and Metastory. - YouTube. Retrieved July 8, 2020, from https://www.youtube.com/watch?v=nsZ8XqHPjI4

100. Anderberg, J. (2020, April 29). 11 Alternatives to the Traditional 4-Year College. Retrieved July 08, 2020, from https://www.artofmanliness.com/articles/is-college-for-everyone-10-alternatives-to-the-traditional-4-year-college/

101. Scholarships for Entrepreneurs. (n.d.). Retrieved July 08, 2020, from http://www.collegescholarships.org/scholarships/business/entrepreneur.htm

102. Thiel, P. (2010). The Thiel Fellowship. Retrieved July 08, 2020, from https://thielfellowship.org/

103. Life After High School: Top 10 Alternatives to College. (2017, July 24). Retrieved July 08, 2020, from https://www.familyeducation.com/teens/life-after-high-school-top-10-alternatives-college

104. Sipek, S. (2017, March 22). 8 alternatives to a 4-year degree. Retrieved July 08, 2020, from

https://www.careerbuilder.com/advice/8-alternatives-to-a-4year-degree

105. Weissmann, J. (2012, April 23). 53% of Recent College Grads Are Jobless or Underemployed-How? Retrieved July 08, 2020, from https://www.theatlantic.com/business/archive/2012/04/53-of-recent-college-grads-are-jobless-or-underemployed-how/256237/

106. Rothwell, J. (2016, December 23). The declining productivity of education. Retrieved July 08, 2020, from https://www.brookings.edu/blog/social-mobility-memos/2016/12/23/the-declining-productivity-of-education/

107. Albright, L. (2018, January 12). 5 smart reasons to abolish the Department of Education. Retrieved July 08, 2020, from https://www.conservativereview.com/news/5-smart-reasons-to-abolish-the-department-of-education/

Made in the USA
Columbia, SC
12 September 2020

20088552R00145